Thoughts from other Authors

"Chances are, if you live on planet Earth long enough, you'll experience at least one life-defining moment where you face something so big, so overwhelming that it feels like you can't go on. This is exactly what happened to middle-school teacher, Renee Haley, and her family one hot August night when a policeman on a house call in their small town of Noble, Oklahoma, made a careless mistake, shooting her five-year-old son, killing him instantly and leaving their lives forever shattered. Here, she recounts the story of that horrible night and shares her path to stepping out of her dark dungeon of grief, sadness, helplessness, anger, and rage, daring to live life and believe in God even when it felt as though she couldn't. So, if you are facing such a tragedy in your life, feel you can't go on, and that if there really is a God, then why would he let this happen to you, this book will help you see a light in your darkness and change your can't into could and your could into a life worth living!"

—DARLEEN BAILEY BEARD,

Award-Winning Children's Book Author

"Renee Haley's moving tale is sure to warm the hearts of any person of faith, especially those dealing with grief. Her story reminds us that no challenge is insurmountable."

—WILLIAM BERNHARDT, author of

The Last Chance Lawyer

"*Tragedy: Confronting the Unthinkable* is a mother's poignant and heartrending true story that pulls readers into the dusty roads of a small American town shaken to its core when a young boy is taken from the safety of his world way too soon, and his unsuspecting family is catapulted into paralyzing loss and grief. This memoir is rife with unparalleled sorrow, coupled with a valiant journey towards justice and a harrowing quest to grant forgiveness to those whom we may not always want to give it. With the turn of every page, readers will embark on a soulful, faith-filled ride, then walk away knowing no tragedy could ever overshadow the goodness and faithfulness of our Almighty God."

"Renee Haley shows remarkable vulnerability as she opens the door to intense personal tragedy and invites the reader to join her on the journey."

"Told with courage and candor, and through the lenses of the *sustenance of hope* and the *beauty of gratitude*, this story chronicles a deep dive into

a family's suffering that will encourage others during their own lonely journeys through loss. This poignant story will compel you to consider the transient nature and preciousness of life, as well as the hard-wired potential of every life, young and old, to have great purpose and lasting impact."

Why, the question asked following a tragedy on this side of Heaven. There is no earthly answer that makes sense. The supernatural impressions and premonitions from a five-year-old boy remind us that Earth is not our home but a temporary dwelling place. Renee Haley shares her pain, God moments, anger, and grief while revealing a trust in God's love. If you have experienced the unthinkable—the loss of a child—this book won't answer your why, but it will provide hope, hope for a future.

—LORI WILDENBERG, author of

Messy Hope: Help Your Child Overcome Anxiety, Depression, or Suicidal Ideation

TRAGEDY

CONFRONTING THE UNTHINKABLE

by

RENEE HALEY

Tragedy: Confronting the Unthinkable

Book Cover by Margarita Rodriguez

Edited by Author Darleen Bailey Beard, Author Brett Nelson, Author Susan Palmer, and Author Dominique Pittenger

Published in the United States of America

ISBN: 9798448655869

Dedication

For my husband, Jack Haley, you have been a tremendous source of encouragement throughout the writing of this book. You are an excellent dad and husband. I love you.

For our children and future grandchildren in memory of our son, Austin Gabriel Haley. Remember to always keep God first in your lives, and He will be your Savior, your hope, and your refuge in times of trouble.

Also, for any person who may be going through an unimaginable situation in your own life. Keep your faith—you can make it through.

Acknowledgments

To my wonderful father, Jack Tracy: You have been an outstanding informational contributor to this book and a wonderful grandpa to our children.

To my mother, Cheryl Tracy, and my mother-in-law, Bettie Haley: Thank you for the many hours and days of editing the manuscript and for being outstanding grandmothers to our children.

To my sister, Michelle Hall: I appreciate the information you contributed to this book and for being an amazing aunt to our children.

To Barbara Allen, Austin's aunt: We appreciate you using your talent as a barber who had cut Austin's hair his entire life and trimmed his hair at the funeral home after his death. It meant so much to us being able to keep hair from his first haircut and also his last.

To each one of our family and friends: We appreciate you lifting us and giving us strength every day through hugs, gifts, flowers, food, cards, or simply using your talents in various ways to encourage and comfort us.

To the countless hundreds of thousands worldwide, including all those in our community who have prayed for us: Your support gave us strength, and your prayers gave us peace. We could not have made it without you.

To all of Austin's dear friends: We love you so much. Thank you for playing with and loving him the way you did. You all have comforted our hearts with your "Gifts of Austin's Remembrance" throughout the years.

To Noble Public Schools, with a special thanks to Katherine I Daily Elementary School, Austin's teacher, Ms. Brown, and her assistant, Ms. Hart: We appreciate the hours you spent loving Austin and teaching him in Pre-K.

To Photographer Stephanie Knowles: Thank you for taking the time to produce our book cover photos.

To Graphic Designer Margarita Rodriguez: Thank you for the amazing book cover, title page, and silhouette graphic.

To my friends who helped edit my manuscript: Authors Darleen Bailey Beard, Brett Nelson, Susan Palmer, and Dominique Pittenger—Thank you for working with me while showing professionalism and sensitivity. It was a difficult book to write, but you helped me through it.

Contents

This poem was written in February 2001, six months before Austin's birth.

HOW VERY OFTEN I HAVE DREAMED OF YOU

How very often I have dreamed of you,
To hold you in my arms,
To kiss you on your cheek,
And to comfort all day long.

How very often I have dreamed of you,
A world of perfect bliss,
To hold your tiny hand in mine,
And give a little kiss.

How very often I have dreamed of you,
My precious boy or girl,
With silky black hair like Daddy's,

Or like Mama's with reddish curls.

How very often I have dreamed of you.
Please, God, keep my baby safe.

I can't wait to hold you in my arms
And gaze into your face.

Renee Haley
Austin's Mama

"I'll love you forever,

I'll like you for always,

As long as I'm living,

My baby you'll be."

—Robert Munsch, *Love You Forever*—

No Reason to Worry

"Mama! This is going to be a very bad day!" Those were Austin's words to me as I woke him just before dawn on Friday, August 3, 2007.

I had a teachers' meeting I needed to attend in our small town of Noble, Oklahoma, so I was waking my boys to prepare them for daycare.

I sat at the end of my five-year-old son's bed, rubbing his back until his eyes opened from a deep sleep.

Stirring from slumber, he laid his head in my lap and looked up at me; his large, brown eyes were serious. Then he made that single declaration, and his voice rattled me. Had he not yet shaken a bad dream?

His alarm seemed peculiar and unsettling, so unlike his usual, "I love you so much, Mama."

I ran my fingers through his soft, brown hair as his statement echoed through my thoughts. Hopefully, his fear would subside as he emerged from his sleep-induced haze, I told myself as I scooped him up in my arms in a playful embrace.

Maybe I could make him laugh and release his worry. Pressing my lips into his cheek, I hoped my love would overflow into my sweet boy's mind and calm his fear.

His warmth and love enveloped me as he placed the sweetest kiss on my cheek. Then, he sank into my early morning cuddles, still heavy with burden.

"Baby, did you have a bad dream?" I whispered in his ear. "We aren't going to have a bad day today. I promise. Mama, Daddy, and your little brother love you so much; everything will be fine. Okay?"

He was silent with apprehension, prompting me to repeat, "Austin, did you have a bad dream? Tell Mama about it."

His emotions kept his words trapped within him, but tears flowed down his face, soaking my shirt.

I tried to swallow my rising anxiety and drew him in tighter, rocking him from side to side in the morning darkness. For the next few minutes, neither of us spoke a word.

On a typical day, I took my young boys for breakfast at our church daycare, but since Austin was so upset, it was better to take our time getting ready and have breakfast at home.

While he ate, he wanted to be near me and watch his favorite cartoons on TV, so I placed his breakfast on the floor as he ate a few more bites. Tears continued streaming down Austin's face, dripping into his cereal bowl. It must be more than a bad dream. Something was wrong. *Very* wrong, so I asked him to sit in my lap and rocked him while asking more questions,

"Son, what's wrong?"

"I don't know," he sobbed.

"Do your friends treat you right at daycare?"

"Yes."

"You like your teachers, don't you?"

"Yes."

"So, you *do* like the daycare and playing with your friends?"

"Yes."

"So, what's wrong, Baby? Tell Mama."

Tears fell from my *own* eyes because he was so upset.

"I don't know what's wrong. I'm just gonna miss you, Daddy, and Dalton so much."

I cuddled and rocked him for another five minutes before he crawled to the floor to finish his cereal.

After getting the kids ready, I took Austin and my younger son to daycare. As I checked them in for the day, Austin began to cry again. How odd. Any other time, he'd run into his classroom without care.

Austin never walked anywhere, especially when he talked and played with his friends. He'd attended this daycare located not far from home for several years, so he knew almost everyone. When I lifted him into my arms that morning, he cried so hard that I began to weep with him. *How could I even consider attending my work meeting with Austin in his current condition?*

Again, I asked him the same question: "Son, *what is wrong?* Why are you upset? It's not like you. There's no reason to worry. Are you okay?" I felt his forehead. It wasn't hot.

"I don't know what's wrong," he sobbed, "but, Mama, I'm going to miss you, Daddy, and Dalton *sooooo* much."

I looked at Kim, the lady at the front desk who always greeted Austin and Dalton with a loving smile and hug. She cried because the two of *us* had tears rolling down our cheeks. I said, "Kim, I don't know why he's crying. He's been upset like this all morning. He woke up saying today was going to be a bad day. I thought he'd had a bad dream or something, but he hasn't stopped crying. I don't know what to do."

Austin asked Kim, "Can I play with Dalton today?"

"Of course!" Kim replied. "We'll find a way to make that happen."

I consoled him even more by asking, "Austin, what do you want to do when we get home today? Want to read some books together? Or watch your favorite movie, *The Adventures of Sharkboy and Lovagirl*? How about playing with Transformers? I'll do anything you want."

He had three wishes. "I want you to push me on the swing, I want to play in the sandbox, and I wanna go to the pond."

I told him we could do all those things, which seemed to make him happier, so I gave Austin and Dalton a kiss goodbye. "Bye-bye, boys. Have a good day. Mama loves you and will see you when my meeting's over!"

A smile crept across my lips as they held hands and rushed down the hallway to their classrooms.

"The Love of a Family is Life's Greatest Blessing"

—Eva Burrows—

A Glance Back at Austin's Life

Oh, this beloved boy of ours. I gave birth to him—a seven-pound two-ounce perfect little boy with brown hair and chocolate-brown eyes on October 24, 2001, at 12:09 in the afternoon. He was the most adorable baby I had ever seen. I know all moms say that, but it was true. Even more amazing, I was his mama. I could hardly believe it.

Minutes after his birth, our families crammed into the tiny hospital room to see our bundle of joy. We gathered in a circle and launched his life of serving Jesus by praying and singing the well-known children's song, *"Jesus loves me, this I know. For the Bible tells me so. Little ones to Him belong. They are weak, but He is strong. Yes,*

Jesus loves me. Yes, Jesus loves me. Yes, Jesus loves me. The Bible tells me so."

With his tiny eyes wide and peering around the room, Austin already knew the name of Jesus.

As he continued his life as a precious baby, a busy toddler, and an active young boy, I began calling him "my little man."

Three years later, Dalton was born. Austin couldn't wait to hold his new baby brother for the first time that September 22, 2004.

The boys exchanged gifts, and Austin was excited to give Dalton a toy hammer he chose with great care. Dalton gave Austin a doctor's kit (with some help from me), and Austin *knew* Dalton had picked it out himself.

At that moment of gift-giving, they became best buds—inseparable from then on. Austin referred to Dalton as "little brother," and when Dalton was old enough, he called Austin "Bubba."

They did everything together—assembled puzzles, played on the swings, battled with plastic swords, played with Hot Wheels, ate meals, watched TV—I mean everything.

One year, Austin wanted to be Batman for Halloween, so it was only natural for Dalton to be the ever-formidable sidekick, Robin. So as we wandered from door-to-door trick-or-treating in our small town, Austin held Dalton's hand and spoke to him with a soft, sweet voice. Dalton adored everything about Austin.

Austin was mature for his age. He quoted Bible verses in church every Sunday evening at four years old.

My husband, Jack, and I loved to watch his relatively tall, slender frame climb the steps to the platform. We marveled at his confidence as he spoke into the microphone that was almost as big as he was.

Tragedy

"My name is Austin Haley, and my Bible verse is—"

His favorite was Jeremiah 17:7. "Blessed is the man who trusts in the Lord, whose confidence is in Him." He seemed to know what that verse meant and often quoted it to family and friends.

As a reward, when he quoted scriptures in church, he and the other kids who quoted their scriptures rummaged through the clear candy box located on a small table on the stage, and often, he came back to the pew with a bright smile and a package of his favorite candy, Skittles.

One time, when I picked up Austin from morning preschool, one of the teachers told me about something she had seen during recess. Her eyes sparkled with amusement as she spoke. "On the playground, he climbed to the highest section of the slide, and he waited for all the other kids to gather. I wondered what he would do next, so I sneaked in a little closer to hear him speaking to them. As several friends clustered around him, he asked, 'Does everybody here know Jesus?'"

"No, I don't know Jesus," a little girl replied.

And that was all Austin needed to hear. Without thinking about it, he rushed to this little girl's side and said, "You need to ask Him into your heart. He's the best superhero of them all!'"

The teacher couldn't believe what she had witnessed, and his advanced ability to speak about Jesus at such a young age amazed her.

On another occasion, after Austin's fifth birthday, he came home from afternoon daycare in his usual state—extremely hungry. As he searched the pantry for a snack, he peered around the open door. "Yes, Mama?"

"Baby, Mama didn't call you," I said, watching TV in the next room.

"Oh, okay." He shrugged and returned to the task at hand, but he glanced around the door again a minute later. "Mama, you keep calling my name. Do you want something?"

It dawned on me what might be happening. Was Austin having an encounter similar to Samuel's experience in the Bible?

"Son, I'm not calling you, but it could be God calling your name, so you need to answer and tell Him you're listening."

Jack, my husband, overheard our conversation and asked, "Hey, Buddy, do you know who Samuel is in the Bible?"

Austin shook his head no.

"Samuel was a young boy—like you. As he fell asleep one night, he heard someone calling his name. '*Samuel. Samuel.*'

"Samuel thought Eli, the man he lived with, called out to him, but it wasn't Eli. So as soon as Samuel laid back and closed his eyes, the voice called him again. '*Samuel.*'"

"Wait—that's what happened to me!" Austin said.

"Yeah, you may be right. Well, someone called Samuel *three* different times, and each time, Samuel went into Eli's room to ask if he called him. After the third time, Eli realized it was *God* who called to Samuel," Jack told him. "And Eli told Samuel that the next time it happened, Samuel should say, 'Speak, Lord, for your servant is listening.'"

Austin's eyes misted over, deep in thought, as he considered the story he'd heard. "Isn't that amazing?" I asked. "God *Himself* spoke to Samuel. He knew Samuel's name, and He knows *your* name, too, Austin." I crouched to my knees in front of him and wrapped my arms around his waist. Looking into his curious brown eyes to make sure he understood the words I spoke, I said, "Next time you hear God calling,

I want you to say the words Eli told Samuel. '*Speak, Lord, for your servant is listening.*'"

"Wow! I bet that *was* God calling me. If *you* didn't call my name, and *Daddy* didn't call my name, it *had* to be God!"

Two weeks before Austin said, "*Today's going to be a very bad day,*" he asked me detailed questions about Heaven. One was, "Mama, how do we get from here to Heaven?"

"It happens this fast." I snapped my fingers. "Some people even say they see a bright light before they pass away."

He appeared to be in deep contemplation, his head at a slight tilt. Then, he grew quiet as he thought about what I'd told him.

Later the same day, as I washed dishes in the kitchen, he mentioned his favorite colors. He loved coloring everything black and gray. "Mama, if you'll look around, almost everything has the colors black or gray on it somewhere."

I glanced around the room at various objects: the table and the chairs in the dining room, the faucet on the kitchen sink, and the picture frame on the wall. Then, as I rinsed another plate and placed it in the dishwasher, I said, "You know, Son, you're right. I never thought about it, but almost everything *does* include the colors black or gray."

My response pleased Austin, and he smiled. Then, his smile fading, he asked another question. "Will the colors black and gray be in Heaven?"

"I'm sure they will."

He named other colors to see if they would be there as well. "Red? Blue? How about yellow 'cause I like yellow. Black and gray will always be my favorites, though."

"Heaven will have a wide array of colors, and we will see every one of them when we get there," I answered.

"Maybe we'll even see colors we don't have here on Earth," I said. "Have you heard of jasper or sapphire? According to the Bible, there will be a wall made of twelve layers in Heaven, and each layer will be a different color. Isn't that awesome?"

His eyes widened because that was new information; he liked learning new things. So, he soaked in every bit of knowledge his hungry mind could hold.

That evening as I helped him to bed, I handed over his soft bear blanket. He liked to rub it between his thumb and first two fingers as he drifted to sleep. The blanket, a gift from Grandma Cheryl, his maternal grandmother, and MaMaw Dixie, his maternal great-grandmother, was always near him.

He rolled to his side. "Mama, can I take my blanket to Heaven?"

"You can have as many blankets in Heaven as you want."

He told me he wanted *that* blanket, so I told him that God could make that happen. A smile sprang across his lips as he said his bedtime prayer and fell fast asleep with his bear blanket clutched in his hands.

A few days later, Austin and I went shopping at Mardel, our local Christian bookstore. Naturally, his first mission was to look at Bibles.

Austin loved Bibles, and he carried his Bible—sometimes more than one—everywhere he went.

I showed him one with pictures, but he had no interest in a children's Bible.

Instead, he picked up one with a camouflage cover. The admiration on his face told me he'd found his heart's desire. I tried to coax him into buying the children's Bible for several minutes, but he said, "Mama, I don't care about pictures. I want to know what the words say."

His words touched my heart, and soon he had yet another Bible to add to his collection.

He clutched his new Bible on the way home, saying, "Now I'm in the Lord's Army."

He treasured that Bible and stared at the map on the back page for hours at a time.

Austin frequently chose healthy foods, and his favorite meals were fish or chicken, apples or peaches, and broccoli. He called the stalks of broccoli "trees." But, unlike most kids his age, he never enjoyed the taste of cake.

Our five-year-old boy had a gentle spirit, and he played with everybody at preschool and daycare. He called them all his best friends and was such a leader the other kids often wanted to follow him.

I remembered when Austin's cousin, Shaylin, had a birthday party and a group of fifteen or twenty girls chased him all over the place. Giggles and laughter echoed throughout the gym when they caught him and knocked him down. Then, when he stood up and took off again, the entire group of girls immediately chased after him. It was funny to me that he liked it when the girls chased him.

I recall many humorous times with Austin, who never wanted to get dirty. We went to my sister's house in the summer, so Austin and his little brother could play with their cousins. Austin and Shaylin, eight months apart, enjoyed playing in the sandbox, digging tunnels in the sand, and building roads. Austin always used the shovels to scoop the sand while Shaylin dug through the mud with her hands.

When Austin was ready to stop digging, he rode a small, motorized four-wheeler while Cooper, his three-year-old cousin, drove. He had not obtained a driver's license yet, so he wove in and out of trees—narrowly avoiding mishap—while pressing the accelerator at top speed. Austin saw Shaylin and requested rescue by reaching out his hand as far as he could toward her saying, "Help! Please, get me out of here!" When Shaylin turned and saw him, she thought he wanted a big high-five, so she gave him a very muddy high-five. Austin didn't know her hands were covered in mud, so when their hands met, he looked at the palm of his hand and wrinkled his nose in utter disgust. *"Eww!"*

He did *not* enjoy getting dirty, and now, he had a glop of wet mud dripping from his hand onto his lap. *Yuck!*

As though nothing had happened, Cooper shot off, full force ahead, like a runaway train while Austin gripped the side of the car for dear life.

My sister and I laughed because we knew of Austin's propensity for the pristine, and we ran to the rescue before Cooper hit a tree. Anytime my sister and I are together, we enjoy reminiscing about that day.

Tragedy

Austin enjoyed all aspects of life, even sports. He played his first season of T-ball during the spring of 2007, and he couldn't wait to run the bases as fast as possible.

Though basketball was still a couple of years away for him, it was the one sport he looked forward to the most.

Austin enjoyed many games and activities, but his favorite was sitting with the family and watching superhero cartoons. He would hold his juice cup in one hand while holding his brother's hand in the other.

When not watching his cartoons, he practiced putting puzzles together. One was a map of the United States. It never ceased to amaze me how he would place each on the floor, always careful to arrange them in one perfect row.

He was a perfectionist.

He would then hold each piece in front of his two-year-old brother as if Dalton knew what he was talking about and say, "Look, Dalton. This shape is Florida, where Mickey and Minnie Mouse live. California is this one. Do you remember Uncle Leonard driving his truck to California?" He showed Dalton every puzzle piece and told a little story behind each one before placing it on the puzzle board. Dalton could repeat a few of the state names after hearing Austin say them many times.

Austin was proud that he, a five-year-old, could complete the puzzle quickly and without help from Mom and Dad, and he hoped Dalton could one day finish the puzzle, too.

It didn't take long for Jack and me to realize Austin learned things faster than most kids his age.

As a public-school teacher, I felt blessed to stay home with my children during summer breaks, and I used each summer to teach Austin how to read and count.

Learning excited Austin, and he always wanted to absorb more information. So, one day, as we sat around the dining room table, he helped me cut pieces of paper large enough to write one word on each of them. The words ranged from one to five letters in length, and we used over one hundred words. I helped him with each one. When done, each piece of paper served as a flashcard until he learned each word.

Every night before I put him to bed, we read through each flashcard. When he read a word without error, we got a piece of tape and put the card on the wall to make a "word train" along his bedroom wall.

By summer's end, he learned one hundred and ten new words, finally reaching the goal he set for himself. He wanted the word train to line up all around his bedroom wall, and before the end of summer, it did.

As any mom could attest, it made me proud to see him accomplish his goal, and many times to reward him for his efforts, I swung him around in circles as we both laughed with delight.

It is a great memory, and I will forever cherish his enthusiasm as he begged, "Mama, I want to learn another word!"

In addition to reading, Austin could count well. So, as I pushed him in the swing, I would count out loud, push by push. Austin would repeat after me, and after reciting to one hundred, he was ready to play something else.

Tragedy

Austin excelled in preschool, and Jack and I were proud parents of a wonderful little boy.

His fantastic pre-kindergarten teacher, Ms. Brown, was impressed with his class participation and advanced abilities. It thrilled us when she suggested he could skip kindergarten and move on to the next grade. We hadn't made the decision yet.

Austin ran everywhere he went, and I always teased him about it. "Son, you learned to walk at ten and a half months, and you ran the next day."

He seemed convinced that's when he learned to run, and I never told him any differently.

Since he loved athletic activities, Austin, Dalton, and I enjoyed playing "tag" around the yard while Jack was at work. Austin could run fast for his age, and it wasn't easy to catch him. One of the sweetest moments was when he tagged Dalton. Austin knew Dalton could never reach him since his little brother was so small, so Austin would pretend to run full speed ahead. In reality, he ran in slow motion, so Dalton could run beside him, stretching as far as his little arm could reach to tag Austin on his back.

"Tag," Dalton exclaimed in his two-year-old voice.

"Oh! You got me, little brother!" Austin replied, smiling, and put his arms around him in an enormous bear hug.

Oh, the bond of these brothers.

In June 2007, I took the boys to Vacation Bible School. Austin especially looked forward to attending each summer with his brother and cousins.

That year, the teachers set up different rooms with various games to teach Bible stories. One of the games was an obstacle course.

Most of the kids struggled to cross the balance beam, the theme of which taught the kids that struggles often happen in life, but we can trust God to help us.

"*On your mark, get set, go!*" Austin's teacher said when he was on the start line.

It only took a few seconds for Austin to complete the course. With swift, deft movements, he navigated over stumbling blocks, dragged himself under part of the course on his stomach, went through the tube, crossed the beam, and finished the entire circuit in seconds.

At the finish line, he proclaimed, "I didn't want the struggles of life to slow me down! God will always help me through." It surprised me when he spoke so maturely, like an adult.

But, now in retrospect, I see he needed, we needed, his big profession of faith to face what was barreling down our pike.

"Be grateful every second of every day
that you get to spend with the people you
love. Life is so very precious."

—Mandy Hale—

Shockwaves of Disbelief

 After finishing my teachers' meeting on that fateful day, I was thrilled to pick up my boys from daycare. I knelt and gave them a big hug as they ran to my open arms, almost knocking me over.

As soon as we entered the front door of our house, Austin said, "I'm going to give *everybody* in my family a hug and a kiss." As he climbed the steps to see Daddy in the computer room, he opened the upstairs door and took a long, silent look at him.

Later, Jack described Austin's face as a look of sadness. It was so uncharacteristic of Austin that Jack wondered if something terrible had happened at daycare.

After Austin looked at him for a few seconds, he said, "I love you, Daddy," and he gave Jack a hug and a kiss.

"I love you too, Son. With all my heart."

Austin came downstairs to the kitchen and wrapped his arms around my waist, squeezing as tight as possible. I hugged him back and kissed the top of his head.

He saw Dalton. "Oh, don't worry, little brother. You get a hug, too." He gave Dalton such a big hug Dalton's foot dangled from the floor. They both giggled. Austin set him down, and they ran down the hallway to play in Austin's room.

Our family left to eat at a restaurant with a buffet a little while later. We had a great meal together. As Austin finished his last few bites of pizza, he reminded me of the promises I made earlier that morning about pushing him on the swing, playing in the sandbox, and going to the pond. I reassured him I had not forgotten. I always looked forward to spending time with my boys.

We returned home around 6:45 p.m. The boys and I went to the swing set in our backyard while my husband retreated to the shop to tend to his hobby of restoring classic cars. I pushed Austin and Dalton on the swing to their hearts' content while Austin practiced counting to one hundred.

In the sandbox, we made castles and used shovels to design rivers and mountains in the wet sand. As we dug, I heard voices at the neighbor's house, but I didn't think much of it as there was a long row of houses stretched in a line behind our property, where children often played in their backyards.

The muffled conversations continued behind a chain-link fence and a narrow strip of trees. I could only hear snippets of the conversation. Something about a snake . . . a fire . . . a hole. I couldn't see the people speaking through the trees.

"Shh, I think somebody needs help with a snake or something. Be quiet for a minute," I whispered to Austin and Dalton. We listened, but silence filled the air, so I assumed the neighbors must have fixed the issue.

The kids were tired and ready to wrap up their play session, so we made our way back to the house.

Once inside, I turned on the TV to one of the boys' favorite shows, *SpongeBob SquarePants*. Austin sat in my recliner drinking juice while Dalton lay on the floor to resume working on the puzzle he and Austin had begun earlier.

Usually, my husband mows our grass on our riding lawn mower, but that night I tackled the task of cutting the front yard with a push mower for a bit of exercise. I pulled my hair into a ponytail, slipped on some gloves, and then pulled the mower to the edge of the grass. I was about to start it when, in the distance, I saw my dad and Papa Jim drive up in Dad's Polaris Ranger, an off-road vehicle with a flatbed in the back. It could mean only one thing: they would ask the boys if they wanted to go to the pond near our house.

I wasn't surprised by the impromptu outing. Since our house sits between my parents' house and our shared pond, it happened at least two or three times a week. That day, it would also conveniently complete Austin's to-do list, so I ran inside to tell the boys.

"Austin! Dalton! Guess what? Grandpa and Papa Jim are here to see if you want to go to the pond!"

Austin jumped out of the recliner, smiling from ear to ear, "Mama, this was my last wish! I can't believe it! Come on, little brother. Let's go!"

Once their shoes were on, I followed them outside to help them climb into the vehicle. I gave them each a quick hug and kiss on their foreheads.

"I hope you have lots of fun! I'm glad you get to feed the fish with Grandpa and Papa Jim," I told them.

My dad leaned in and gave me a sweet kiss on the cheek. "Honey, why don't you go to the pond with us?"

I shook my head. "I'd love to, Dad, but I think I'll mow the front yard first if you and the kids don't mind. It shouldn't take me more than twenty minutes. After that, I'll meet you there."

"Yay! Mama's comin'!" Austin and Dalton cheered. Their eager smiles said it all. They could barely wait for the fun to begin.

"We'll see you in a little while," Dad said.

"I'll be there as soon as I finish the front yard," I promised.

The outstanding fisherman he was, Papa Jim held the fish food bucket and a fishing pole. A container of worms was in his lap. I told him, "I hope you can help the boys catch a two or three-pound catfish today."

Papa Jim smiled, always seeming to enjoy showing the boys how to catch fish.

I waved goodbye, and off they drove to the pond.

The air was cool on my face, which was unusual. Oklahoma Augusts are notoriously sweltering, but that night was in the low eighties, a nice reprieve from the relentless hot temperatures and humidity.

Our water hose was still out, stretched across the yard, so I rolled it up, humming to the music playing in Jack's shop. I stopped humming, though, when I heard the return of the muffled voices from the neighbor's backyard. I still couldn't hear all they were saying, but I could tell it was a conversation between a few people. Then I heard them shout more clearly, "Fire in the Hole!"

Is something on fire? I wondered. Earlier, I had heard them speaking of a snake and a hole. I was trying to make sense of it all. I looked in the sky for smoke, but I didn't see any signs of fire. Then, I heard the people at the neighbor's house laughing, and all my worries left me.

Then I heard my boys giggling.

It wasn't uncommon for them to receive a shower or two from the large catfish when they jumped out of the water, and the boys always thought it was hilarious when their clothes got soaked from unexpected waves. Just imagining the scene made me smile.

I walked over to the lawnmower, started the engine, and made a couple rounds of cut grass.

About five minutes later, I heard a loud *BOOM!* The vibration was so loud, it made me tremble. I released the bail bar, silencing the mower into an eerie silence. *Was that a gunshot?* I glanced at my watch. It was about 8:05 p.m.

I quickly launched into silent prayer for whoever shot the gun. "Lord, please let that person be okay."

Is my family okay? I wondered. The muscles in my arms tensed. I paused, listening for unusual noises. Finally, I thought I heard my dad shout, "We're okay down here!" so I restarted the mower and began another lap even though my heart pounded so hard I could barely breathe.

About six seconds later, there was another loud, teeth-rattling BOOM!

Again, my body vibrated from the sound, and my mind filled with anger. *Whoever is doing this should know better than to shoot a gun inside city limits. What is going on? Who is discharging a firearm this close to my home?*

As I turned the corner of my front yard with the lawn mower to get a better look, my dad's Polaris raced in my direction.

At first, it relaxed me to know they had come home safely. *Wait. Why are they coming back already? They'd only been gone less than ten minutes.* I jumped back a step or two as my dad's vehicle pulled rapidly into our driveway, almost hitting me.

"Austin! Someone sh—shot him. Austin!" Dad gasped.

The roar of the lawnmower combined with the rumble of the Polaris muffled my dad's words into a slur of vague and indiscernible mumblings. "What?" I asked.

I released the bail of the lawn mower to silence the motor once again. It seemed to take forever for the deafening sound to end.

"It's Austin! He's been shot! I don't think he's going to make it!"

"What? I said, my heart pounding. *Did he say what I thought he said? Surely not. No. He couldn't have.* "Wh—what did you say?" It took tremendous effort to speak the words.

Once again, he repeated the statement, and his words exploded like a bomb in front of my face, "Honey, someone shot Austin—right in the head—I don't think he's going to make it— I'm so sorry!" He shook his head in disbelief.

My eyes began a frantic search for Austin. Dalton was in the front seat with my dad, but *where was Austin? Where was Papa Jim?*

I broke into a sprint toward the pond.

Nooooooo!" I screamed. "Noooooooooo!" *This can't be real!*

"Austin, Mama's coming! Mama is coming! Mama is here!"

I was twenty feet from the Polaris when my husband, Jack, heard my frantic shrieks and came running.

Obviously, he hadn't heard the gunshot due to the blaring music. Placing a firm hand on my shoulders, he gave me a gentle shake. "What's wrong? Tell me! What's wrong?"

The fear in his eyes made it impossible to speak with ease.

I was gasping, and each word caught in my throat. "Someone . . . shot Austin . . . while . . . he was . . . at the pond!" As the words came out, I wasn't sure they were mine. *Did I say someone shot our son?* I trembled as if an earthquake were rising from my inner being. My head felt like it could explode. *This can't be. This has to be a mistake—a big, big mistake.*

Jack and I took off toward the pond, but my dad's following shout stopped us. "Noooooo! Don't go down there! The shooter may still be there! Austin's here with me! In the back of the Polaris!" Though my dad had shouted these words before, my mind would not—could not—comprehend his words due to the fear and the intense level of anxiety within me. Finally, I understood.

We rushed to the back of the vehicle. Jack got there before I did and collapsed to his knees. He attempted to get back to his feet but couldn't.

"What happened? Tell me! What happened?" he yelled numerous times.

Dalton sat in the front seat with my dad. As he heard Jack yelling, he placed his hands over his ears, screaming, "No, Bubba! Nooooo!"

Between Jack's and Dalton's screams, I was in shock.

I ran to the back of my dad's Polaris, took one look at Austin, and lost it. There was a massive hole in his forehead, and blood splattered his face. I yelled, "*Noooooo! Nooooooooo! Not My Baby! Austin, stay with me. Please, don't die!*"

I fell to my knees, weeping and screaming. Sweat poured from my forehead; my muscles clenched from head to toe. My heart seemed to pound out of my chest.

As my eyes met my dad's, I pleaded with him to help. He lifted his bloodstained arms and hands in disbelief, himself. I couldn't think.

I couldn't move. I froze in fear, then heard a howling sound escape my lips—a moaning so deep, so broken, I wasn't even sure it was coming from me.

"This can't be happening! My baby! Wait! Where's . . . Papa Jim? Is he safe?"

"He's still searching for the shooter," Dad said. "He's still there, determined to find whoever did this."

Shooter. Shooter. The words sank into my soul. *Someone shot my baby? But who would do such a horrible thing? Why would someone shoot my five-year-old boy?*

As Jack cried, still on his knees, pleading in anguish, my eyes were drawn to my dad's bloody arms and hands. I watched him pull Dalton closer to him on the front seat, trying to soothe his screams.

Spinning. Spinning. It felt as though a centrifugal force was whipping me around in vicious circles. In the midst of all the screaming, spinning, and howling, my dad shouted for someone to call 911 for an ambulance.

Finally, something clicked. *Ambulance. Ambulance. Yes, ambulance!*

Desperate to stay by my son's side, I knew calling an ambulance was the best way to help him. I took off my gloves and threw them on the ground. I grabbed Dalton from my dad's arms and ran inside the house to make the call.

It seemed as if, even though I ran at full speed, I got nowhere fast. I was determined, however, to protect him.

I blasted through the front door, holding Dalton, and searched for my phone in a state of total panic. *Phone. Phone. Where's my phone?*

"Dalton, I'm sorry. I've got to put you down. I can't find my phone!"

I screamed in sheer frustration, running from room to room, looking for my phone, Jack's phone, *any* phone. I grabbed Dalton's hand to keep him near me and safe.

I searched the side table next to my recliner in the living room, my purse on the kitchen counter, my dresser in the bedroom. Each passing second felt like a lifetime. *Where's a phone? A phone?*

Finally, I found our bedroom phone, which had fallen off the nightstand and hid under the bedspread. My fingers flew over the keypad, dialing 911.

My eyes remained locked on Dalton the entire time.

I sat on the edge of the bed, crying.

Actual 911 RECORDING, August 3, 2007, 8:12 p.m.

Renee (screaming as the phone rang): *"Oh Lord, help us . . . help us! No! No!"*

Operator: *"Noble 911"*

Renee: *"Oh, please help us* (gave address). *Someone just shot my son, and we think he's dead."*

Operator: *"Okay, is there anyone there right now?"*

Renee: *"Yes, my two-year-old son. My five-year-old got shot!"*

Operator: *"Who shot him?"*

Renee: *"Someone for no reason . . . at the pond out by our house."*

Operator: *"You don't know who did it?"*

Renee: *"No, my dad took him to the pond to go fishing, and someone shot him."*

Operator: *"Okay, I am going to keep you on the line. Okay, ma'am?"*

Renee: *"Oh, God, help us! Help us!"* (Speaking to my son) *"Come here, Baby. Come here. It is okay; it's okay, Baby. It's okay. Mama's so scared,*

Baby. I know you are, too. But, oh, God, please help us. Hurry, hurry, hurry! Oh, God, please help us!"

Operator: *"We're coming. Okay, ma'am? Stay right there."* (Placed on hold).

Renee: *"Oh, God . . . Jesus . . . help us! Come here, Dalton"* . . . (Dalton was crying). *"Shh, please pray for your brother . . . please pray. Oh, God, no . . . please, no . . . no, no, no . . . please, Lord, help us. Help us, God. Help us, Jesus. Help us!"*

Operator: *"Are you still there, ma'am?"*

Renee: *"Yes."*

Operator: *"Is he breathing? Is he doing okay?"*

Renee: *"We don't know. My dad came up and told us that he got shot for no reason, and he thinks he's dead."*

Operator: *"Okay."*

Renee: *"Please send an ambulance now!"*

Operator: *"Okay, I'm trying to."*

Renee: *"Oh, God, please help him . . . please."*

Operator: *"Okay, stay calm. Okay? We are sending the helicopter right now. So, stay with us."*

Renee: *"Okay, please hurry . . . please!"*

Operator: *"Stay with him. Are the officers there?"*

Renee: *"No . . . oh, God, help us. Lord Jesus, help us. Come here, Dalton. The officers are here now."*

Operator: *"Okay, I am going to get off the phone with you. Go talk to them. Okay?"*

Renee: *"Okay."*

I picked up Dalton, who was crying and scared, and ran outside to our front yard.

To my surprise, Papa Jim was standing there. "Did you find out who did this to Austin? I pleaded. Who? Tell me, who?"

"No. I couldn't . . . couldn't find anyone!" Papa Jim's eyes darted from side to side, and his breathing was rapid.

Just then, two police officers, a male and a female, appeared on our front lawn.

I ran toward the male officer. I grabbed each of his shoulders and shook him, "You've got to find out who did this to my son! You've got to find out who did this!"

"We will, we will," he assured me. "We have a pretty good idea of who did it."

"*Who?*" I demanded. "Who would do this to my innocent five-year-old boy?"

Instead of telling me or consoling me, he said, "You need to get over there and take care of your son." I was confused by his tone of voice. *If he knows who did this, why isn't he telling me? Why isn't he helping us?*

I ran to Austin, who was still lying in the back of the Polaris.

I sought signs—any signs that he was still alive. I looked at his tiny face. His eyes were half-open as if crying out for help. I held his little hand in mine and wrapped my fingers around his.

I looked at the shirt Austin wore, praying to see the rise and fall of his breathing. The shirt, his favorite *Captain America* shirt, was splattered with mud.

Is his chest moving? Was that a breath?

Through panic-filled gasps, I repeated over and over, "Austin! Keep breathing, Baby. It's Mama. Keep breathing. Can you hear me? Answer me. Squeeze my hand!"

I was desperate to hold him, to rock him as I did earlier in the day, but I was afraid to move him.

I leaned over and gave him a cautious hug, with his face next to mine.

"Mama's here, Baby—Mama's here. Oh, God, help us!"

In an instant, I realized it wasn't mud on his shirt—it was blood—*his blood*—and now it was all over my shirt. His blood covered my hands and my cheek.

Tragedy

Praying for answers, I cast my eyes to the darkening sky. *God, how do I fix this? Is he still alive? Help him be alive.* I looked for the rise and fall of his chest. *Is that a movement? Please, God. Let Austin's chest move. Help him still be alive.*

I stared at his chest. *Is it moving? Did he just breathe? Oh, God, let that be a breath.*

"Austin, this is Mama. Stay with me, Baby! Breathe, breathe!" I screamed, hoping he could hear me.

"God, I can't help him! You parted the Red Sea. You made the lame walk and the blind see. Help my son! Please, pleeaassee, bring my son back to me! God, you can do anything! Please, take away all his pain!"

A deep wailing cry caught my attention, growing louder and louder. It took a few seconds to realize the cry was coming from me, and I couldn't stop. *Why? Why? Why did this happen? Who would shoot my little boy?*

An ambulance sped up our driveway, jolting me back to reality. A paramedic jumped out, pulling a blue gurney from the back. He raced to Austin's side. The second paramedic helped him get Austin out of the Polaris and laid him on the gurney, pressing a stethoscope against Austin's neck. "I think I hear a faint heartbeat."

I hoped and prayed for that heartbeat.

"Ma'am? Ma'am? We need to take your son to the hospital. The dispatcher has already contacted *Med Flight*. They're meeting us at the high school football field about a block away. We have to hurry!"

I nodded even though much of what he said didn't register. *Did he say hospital? Football field?*

"With a gunshot wound to the head, your son has lost a tremendous amount of blood, so we've got to hurry. In the meantime, you and your family can drive to the Norman Regional Hospital Emergency Room. We will meet you there."

"God surely listens, understands, and knows the hopes and fears you keep in your heart. For when you trust in his love, miracles happen."

—Unknown Author—

Fear of the Unknown

Papa Jim took Dalton to his house while my husband, dad, and I headed to the hospital fifteen minutes away. En route, we rushed through as many phone calls as possible, notifying family, but were still unable to reach my mom, the one I needed most.

In all the years I'd been her daughter, she had never failed to be an endless source of encouragement, faith, and love when I needed it. My mom could make everything better, or at least provide me with comfort.

Mom was at the church practicing music for the song service on Sunday, Dad told me, so he dropped Jack and me off at the hospital, then dashed off to get Mom.

Jack and I burst through the hospital entrance, frantic and out of breath. My sister, Michelle, had arrived minutes before us. I sped toward her and collapsed in her arms.

"Michelle, do you know anything?"

"No, nothing, I'm sorry."

Tears ran down her face as she held me in her arms. Jack collapsed to the floor. Michelle helped him to his feet, and we all continued to cry, trying to make sense of what had just happened.

Empty chairs filled the waiting area. The emergency room was eerily silent. *Shouldn't there be a ton of commotion trying to save my son's life? Where is he?* In the corner of my eye, I saw a custodian changing a trash bag. He had a smile on his face. *How are you smiling right now?* Somehow, his smile fueled my rage. *Someone shot my son! Someone shot my son!*

I ran to the lady at the front desk, gasping and drenched in sweat, working hard to bring my panicked breathing under control.

"I can't wait. Please. Our son. Austin Gabriel Haley. He got shot. Where is he? I have to see him."

The lady went through a series of keystrokes on her keyboard. "*Hmm,* I don't see anybody by the name of Austin Gabriel Haley in the hospital right now." She shuffled through the stacks of paperwork that littered the floor beneath her desk.

I shook and trembled, my mind racing with thoughts. *He has to be here! This is where the paramedics said to meet him.*

"What do you mean no one by that name is here? The helicopter picked him up, and they said they brought him here," I told her. "They should have already been here! Find my son! We need to see him —*now!*"

She snatched up her phone, saying, "I'll make some calls to track their location, and we'll also arrange a private waiting room for your family."

Confused, I turned to Jack. "Jack, where is he—where is our son?" I collapsed in his arms.

Jack also asked the lady. "Where's our son? Tell us now! Which room is he in?" He was angry—we both were.

I reached across the desk to shake the lady's shoulders to make her tell me where our son was, but everything began spinning. I felt nauseous, and before I could reach her shoulders, I passed out.

The next thing I knew, I was on the cold, tiled floor, scooting backward and moaning. Tears continued to flow. The sobs wracked my body—barely allowing a breath to be drawn.

Someone placed a wet, cold washcloth across my forehead. I was still moaning. I must have passed out again.

I woke up on the floor in a new room. Our private waiting room.

My husband and sister were there with me.

A doctor rushed through the door. I looked up the best I could, but the room, the lights, the people, everything whirled in vicious circles.

The lights on the ceiling were so bright, they took over my entire vision. Jack grabbed the doctor by the arm, demanding to know about our son.

The doctor touched my shoulder and spoke in a calm voice. "I am so sorry, but . . . he, um, he didn't make it. There was nothing my staff or I could do to help. Again, I am so sorry." He glanced at our family with friendly, sad eyes, but his words hung in the air.

It can't be true, I thought. *How could something so awful be true?* My mind felt foggy, like I wasn't thinking clearly.

Jack fell to his knees and wrapped his arms around me. The doctor repeated, *"There was nothing we could do to help. Again . . . I'm so sorry."*

And the doctor walked out of the room.

Jack and I sobbed and clung to each other. The whole situation just didn't feel real. *How could this be happening to us? To our son?*

I was still on the floor sobbing when my parents entered the hospital room. I barely got the ghastly words out of my mouth. "Mama . . . he . . . didn't . . . make it!" and my mom fell to her knees, wrapped her arms around me, and wept.

My mother-in-law, Bettie, rushed into the room. With a look of anguish, she took Jack in her arms. "I'm so sorry, Son, I'm so sorry! I'm so sorry!"

The nightmare was unbearable not only for us but also for our entire family who assembled that night. All of our family huddled together, comforting each other, crying. My dad, however, was despondent and drenched in Austin's blood from head to toe. Tears streaked his cheeks.

I could only imagine what guilt and extreme pain he must have felt at that moment, so I hefted my body, heavy as bricks, from the floor and sat next to him on the couch. I wrapped him in a tight embrace while resting my head on his shoulder. Jack sat next to me.

I did my best to reassure him. "Dad, it's not your fault. Austin loved going to the pond. It was one of his favorite things."

Tragedy

My dad cradled me in his blood-stained hands and wept harder than I had ever seen him weep. He had always been the strong one, the leader who always knew what to do in any situation. Now, here he was, not knowing what to do and crying hysterically.

I hugged him tightly.

Through the intensity of his tears, my dad spoke. "God bless you for feeling that way. God bless you both." Then he proceeded to tell us what happened on the dock. He sensed we needed every detail, even though it was horrifying to hear.

"Austin, Dalton, Papa Jim, and I had fed the fish," my dad began. "Everything was peaceful and perfect. Austin and Dalton watched the fish surface and splash in search of food. Austin wanted to catch one, so Papa Jim stood behind him and helped put a worm on his hook. A loud *BOOM* rattled the ground and air around us."

My dad shook his head as his mind recalled the scene, and his voice wavered in emotion. "A . . . a . . . bullet flew between my legs and hit the water in front of me. Water splashed into the air. I yelled as loudly as I could, 'Hey! Quit shooting! We're down here!'"

I covered my heart. "I thought I heard you scream, 'Everybody is okay down here!'" I said, my mind still foggy.

"No," my dad said. "The bullet trajectory was so close that my pant legs moved. Dalton took off running, clutching his hands over his ears, and Papa Jim ran off after him. So, I reached around and pulled Austin close to me. I looked around, trying to see where the bullet could've come from.

"Only a few seconds after the first shot, the second shot happened, and it was as loud as a cannon," my dad said in numb disbelief. "I looked at Austin because he had fallen from my arms. He was . . . he was on the dock, blood gushing from his forehead."

My dad's words made my entire body tense up. I couldn't stand the thought of my little boy in such a condition, so I clenched my hands, squeezed my eyes closed, and braced for the next part of the story. I didn't want to hear it, but I needed to know every detail, regardless of how painful it was.

"It looked like he raised his head and looked at me as if saying, 'Please help me, Grandpa.' Blood continued to pour from his forehead. What could I do?"

My dad paused, and he lowered his head toward the floor. I was afraid he wouldn't be able to continue, but he did. "He looked at me with his head resting on the dock, and he died. I felt so helpless."

I tightened my grasp around my dad as he recanted the nightmarish story in a grave voice. "Papa Jim brought Dalton back to the dock, and Dalton took a long look at Austin. As he stood over his brother, he had a puzzled look on his face. I didn't know what to do or say. Dalton looked up. I thought he was looking at me. Instead, he was looking into the sky with a look of awe on his face." My dad remarked about it, but I was too upset for his words to register. Later, however, it would prove to be healing for our entire family, especially Dalton.

Fury coursed through my mind. *What kind of maniac would shoot an innocent five-year-old?* A thought crossed my lips. "Dad, since you're an attorney, do you think an angry client from the opposing side of one of your cases might have done this?"

"I don't know. Maybe. I feel hurt and angry . . . and I am killing mad."

Tragedy

I know my dad well enough to know he would never kill anyone, but I grasped his hand because I understood and felt the emotions behind the statement.

"I couldn't figure out who killed Austin," my dad said, "but I knew I needed to get him to the hospital fast. I thought maybe there was still hope to save his life. 'God, spare Austin,' I prayed. 'Heal this terrible wound.'"

I heard the quiet sniffles of others in the room as they listened in desperation to my dad's recitation, but my attention remained wholly on him.

"I picked up Austin and placed him under my left arm in a bear hug," my dad continued. "Austin's little arms dangled as I lifted him in front of me. His blood ran into my shoes and down my arms. I was desperate."

I stared at my dad's blood-stained arms and knew how difficult it must have been for Dad to hold Austin with one arm because he'd had a stroke eight months earlier and had lost the strength in his right arm and shoulder.

As I listened, I wondered how he held Austin's weight and knew it must have been strength from God. I was thankful my dad could lift him from the dock because the thought of Austin being alone in such a condition would have broken my heart. Dad did everything he could to help my son, and I'll forever love him for that.

"Papa Jim roamed the perimeter in search of the killer. I used my body as a shield between Dalton and the place where we thought the gunshots came from. I didn't want them to shoot Dalton, too.

"I held Austin facing outward, and his body fell over my left arm. I took Dalton's hand with my other. I did my best to position my body between where I thought the bullet came from and Dalton as we struggled up the bank of the pond. Finally, I heaved Austin into the bed of the Polaris. I could barely do it; I could barely lift him because I was so weak, but there was no other choice.

"I headed for you and Jack as fast as I could, and all the way to your house, I was wondering how to tell you that you gave me a bright, healthy grandson, and I brought him back with a bullet in his head.

I . . . didn't know how to tell you and cringed with dread at the prospect.

"I'm so sorry," Dad cried. I wish it were me instead of my grand-baby. If I ever find out who did this, I'll kill him."

I brushed tears from my eyes. Oh my, how hard that had to have been for my dad, and how angry he must have felt. We shared the same emotions. He loved Austin so much. I remember him saying on several occasions, "Austin, you're the apple of my eye."

The bond between Austin and my dad had always been so special.

By the time Dad finished his horrific story, my mom couldn't handle the intense grief; she had burst into tears. I went over to her, wrapped my arms around her, and she pulled me into her lap. We both wept loudly. Everyone wept loudly, and everything was intense. Too intense.

"My baby! My Austin! I need him!"

"I know, Baby," my mom said, "If I could take your pain away right now, I would."

I realized she had her pain, too. She loved Austin as much as I did.

Tragedy

Throughout our hours of grief and misery, a crucial unanswered question still loomed, the haunting focus of all our conversations.

Who killed Austin? Who killed our boy? I remembered something the police had told me when they arrived at our house. Something about how they thought they knew who did it? But, where were the police? Why weren't they telling us who did this? And why weren't they arresting this person?

The turmoil of not knowing who was capable of such a horrendous act was incomprehensible. The anxiety and fear overwhelmed us.

As we sat in the private family room of the hospital, waiting to hear something, the reality of our situation set in like an ominous cloud. I needed Austin with me—I needed him alive, healthy, and happy like all the other boys his age.

The thoughts brought a tidal wave of anguish.

I wept—I screamed—I crawled on all fours in desperate, agonizing prayer.

I laid on my back trying to lock my eyes on one thing to steady my breathing, but the lights, the ceiling, the walls, the people—everything whirled around me like a kaleidoscope and went black.

When I regained consciousness, reality hit me again. I felt like I would vomit.

My heart pulsated so hard in my chest I could hear it roar in my ears. My body trembled, and I became drenched with sweat from head to toe.

My thoughts were a whirlwind. I needed to know who shot and killed my little boy, and I needed to know *now*.

The answers that soon came, however, defied any of our expectations.

"I hate feeling lost without you, like there is a gaping hole here in my heart. It really hurts."

—Unknown Author—

The Explosive Reality

The hours following the shooting were excruciating for the family and me. Finally, at 11:30 p.m. that evening, the Noble police chief and the assistant police chief made their way into our private family waiting room.

The police chief stood for a few seconds before speaking. Inside the doorway, he removed his hat. His eyes swept across the hospital floor tiles before regarding each person in the room.

"What I am about to tell you is very difficult," he said with a gentle tone of authority. "But, we think . . . we know who shot your son."

His ominous words brought overwhelming anticipation.

"Who?" I asked, desperate to know the answer.

The chief took a deep breath and shifted his weight from one foot to the other.

"Unfortunately, we, uh, we believe one of our very own police officers shot the gun."

Gasps and exclamations of disbelief echoed throughout the room. We all glanced at each other, wondering if we had heard correctly.

Astonished at such an unexpected admission, a lump formed in my throat. I could hardly frame my next sentence.

"What? A police officer shot our son? Why?" As much as I tried, I couldn't wrap my mind around such a preposterous idea. *A police officer shot my son? A police officer?*

The chief cleared his throat and, with a subtle nod, continued, "Our officers were called to your neighbor's house about a snake in a birdhouse. Three officers arrived at the residence, and they launched into a discussion about how best to remove the snake from the birdhouse." Again, he shifted his weight from one foot to the other and scanned the floor. The male supervising officer issued the order for one of our other officers to shoot the snake, so he did. He hasn't been working for our department for too long. Unfortunately, there wasn't a good backdrop other than a thin line of trees. And, well, the bullet traveled between the trees and hit your son in the back of the head, from five hundred feet away."

Jack and I looked at each other, unable to believe what we had just heard. "What?" Jack demanded. "A snake? Your officer killed my son because of a *snake*?"

"Um . . . a snake hung from a birdhouse in the neighbor's backyard .

. . and the officers determined shooting it would be the best method to get rid of it."

We still could not fathom what we just heard. "Wait. *What?*"

The chief cleared his throat yet again. "When the three officers heard Renee's screams after the two shots, two of the officers jumped over the neighbor's chain-link fence to see if they could help. The police officer who shot the gun wasn't one of them. They realized their misjudgment in dealing with the situation which resulted in the shooting of your son."

I couldn't take it anymore. In an instant, Austin's premonitions had crystallized into this reality. I screamed at the police officer, "I cannot believe the police officers took my son away from me!

"I want you to listen to me—listen to me carefully right now!—Austin had recurrent *nightmares* for the last three years about police officers taking him away from Jack and me. Do you hear me? Do you hear what I am saying?

"For three years, Austin had recounted that, in his nightmares, we would be happily walking on the side of the road holding his hand with Jack on one side and me on the other, swinging him high in the air. Suddenly, police officers would appear and *strip* him from our arms.

"Austin said the officers would take him and throw him in the back-seat of the police car, and he would pound his fists on the back window as hard as he could for our help.

"In his dream, Jack and I would run as fast as we could to save him, but we couldn't catch up to the car. And now it has manifested—your police *did* take him away from us! We always tried to help him realize he was safe. But he wasn't safe, was he? How dare your police officers be so senseless over a snake? It was only a snake! Why did my son have to die over a snake?"

I continued before the police chief could say a word. "Austin said we were never able to save him in his horrible nightmares. Jack and I consoled Austin the best we knew how and said, 'Police officers are our friends. They help us when needed. They won't hurt you, Austin.'"

I broke into a sob. I couldn't take the realization of his nightmare. "But, they *did* hurt him! Why did the police take my son away from us?"

The chief and the assistant chief both turned white as a sheet. I could tell they were shocked about Austin's recurrent nightmares. I can't recall the other words they said. Their words didn't matter anymore. Austin was gone. *Gone forever.* Austin's nightmare continued cycling through my mind as the police chief issued his final apologies, then he and his assistant departed the room.

I sat next to Jack and glanced at our family around the room. I could see the pain, the anger, and the shock on everyone's faces. We didn't know what to say or do to make the pain disappear.

I put my head in my hands and wept.

That's when I shockingly remembered Austin's words from that very morning.

Mama, this is going to be a very bad day. "Austin was right when he said this was going to be a very bad day. How? How did he know?"

Jack shook his head in disbelief. "Yeah, and do you remember how he asked you all of those questions about Heaven—Can I take my blanket to Heaven? What colors will be in Heaven? Our eyes met and froze. Did God allow Austin to know he was about to die or something?"

74

Tragedy

As we continued discussing the shock of Austin's premonitions, a nurse walked into the room and told us we could see him. Finally.

As we walked the long, cold hallway, I couldn't stand the thought of living life without our sweet son. His words about Heaven and it going to be a very bad day continued swarming my thoughts. With each step, my emotions escalated.

Sadness fell from my eyes as I entered the emergency room, where he lay on the gurney. I couldn't believe it was him lying there.

"My son—I was playing with you in the backyard only a few short hours ago." It was impossible to reconcile.

My parents stepped inside with us. The nurse walked out, closing the blue curtain for privacy. We all wanted to spend time with him—wanted him to respond with signs of his precious life. He was too still, and I found myself searching for movement. He no longer had blood on his face. It was almost as though he were asleep, and he would awaken at any moment. His eyes were still partially open. I wanted him to be alive and needed a miracle. The emergency room nurses had wrapped white gauze around his head to hide the tragic gunshot wound.

In turn, each of us kissed him on the cheek and whispered tearful goodbyes. His short life was forever gone.

But how could I say goodbye? I would never again hold my son in my arms. I couldn't accept such a thought, so I pushed it to the back of my mind to inevitably fester.

I placed my head across his chest. He still felt warm against my cheek, but I no longer heard his precious life-affirming heartbeat. The silence was deafening.

For some surprising reason and because we were still in shock, the family broke into Austin's favorite song, *Jesus Loves Me, This I Know.*

Tears streamed down our faces. I could hardly sing with my chin shaking uncontrollably and my tears flowing non-stop. Still, I sang with all my heart, just in case his spirit was near.

My body was tense with the emotional storm of the past few hours. Yet, as I sang, I remember thinking, *we sang this song not long ago on the day of his birth, and now we sing it again at his death.*

One moment in time can change everything.

The Norman Police Department took over Austin's case, and two officers came from around the closed curtain of the emergency room.

They asked to speak to my dad in the hallway, so my mom went with him. They interrogated him with such questions as "You had a gun at the pond, didn't you?"

"No, I didn't," my dad responded.

"We already checked, and you own guns."

"Yes, I own guns, and they are locked up in a gun safe at home. Do you want me to show them to you?"

"No, but you let people hunt down there, don't you?"

"No, I absolutely don't."

"Well, you don't have it posted, do you?" as if to say that since my dad didn't have it posted, he caused someone to shoot Austin. My dad was devastated.

"I didn't know I needed it posted. We live directly inside city limits, where many houses are lined up and down the street. There is no reason to post inside of city limits and in the middle of a neighborhood."

It was difficult for him to answer some of their pointed questions. They already knew who caused Austin's death, the Noble police officer, so why would they need to ask such questions? It added to the hurt we already felt.

My mom stopped the absurdity. She got in the police officers' faces and yelled, "There is no reason to ask him this! We already know who shot him!"

"Ma'am, Ma'am, this is part of the investigation, so we have to ask these questions."

"Why? You already know who did it, and now you are trying to blame my husband? This is wrong! So wrong!"

"We're going to need you to step outside, so we can ask a few more questions."

They continued the interrogation behind a closed door a few more feet down the hallway.

The officers also interrogated Papa Jim. They asked him the same set of questions.

As Papa Jim spoke to the police, a nurse came into Austin's room and whispered that other family and friends were waiting to see us in the cafeteria. She also explained it was time to send his body to the medical examiner's office.

The police officer who walked in with her said, "I'm sorry, but your parents' house and your house are considered crime scenes, so you won't be allowed to enter your house until we complete our investigation."

"Why are you saying this to us now while we're saying our goodbyes to our son?" I asked, looking up. "I can't even think about that right now."

The officer and the nurse exited the room.

Jack and I leaned over the bed and gave Austin one more kiss goodbye on the cheek. I told him how much we loved him and missed him.

How do I give my baby a final kiss goodbye? The inexplicable loss made me feel overwhelmingly alone. He should be with me, holding my hand, safe and sound, not carted away on a cold hospital gurney.

I would never again hold his hand, with his tiny fingers overlapping mine, and the thought made me tremble from head to toe.

As Jack and I made our way to family and friends, I almost fainted once again, but Jack's hands around my waist brought strength.

Many people waited in the cafeteria to offer words of encouragement and prayer. Both sides of the family were there, along with many wonderful friends.

God bless our family and friends who waited with us until two-thirty in the morning. In total, nearly one hundred people came to the hospital to support our family in a time of need. I don't think anyone will ever realize how much this meant to us because we didn't have to grieve alone.

My body was weak, tired, and exhausted as I contemplated how different our lives would be from here on out. The thought of living without Austin filled my mind with fear. *I can't do this! I can't go on without Austin.*

More than once, I remember praying that all of this was nothing more than a terrible nightmare from which I would soon awaken.

The next step was excruciating. The investigation had finally stopped, so we could go home. But, how could we? We didn't want to leave without our son. But, we had no choice. We had to leave the hospital without our precious boy saying, "Mama and Daddy, I love you."

Our hearts broke. How could we go home without Austin?

His little voice echoed through my mind. "Mama, Daddy, help me!" But we couldn't help him. We wanted to, but there was nothing else we could do.

By the time we picked up Dalton from Papa Jim and MaMaw's house, it was 2:45 a.m.

My sister's husband, Chad, had stayed with Dalton, so MaMaw and Papa Jim could be with us at the hospital.

Our two-year-old Dalton had been asleep for quite some time, but he opened his sleepy eyes long enough to ask, "Daddy, is Bubba okay?"

Our hearts grieved for Dalton. His big brother—his best friend, the one he laughed with, learned from, and played with every day—was *gone*. Forever.

"Shh, go back to sleep," Jack whispered. "We'll talk about it in the morning."

He laid his head on Jack's shoulder and fell back to sleep in his daddy's arms.

When we arrived home and laid Dalton in his bed, he was fast asleep.

As we looked around the house, Austin's half-completed puzzle still lay on the floor, and our TV was still tuned to his favorite channel.

I ran my fingertips over his much-loved teddy bear blanket, which lay on the couch where he had cuddled his little brother.

How lonesome and lost we felt at that moment, but the most challenging step was yet to come. The following morning would require us to find the words to tell Dalton his "Bubba" was gone, out of his life forever.

On the day God took you home
I thought I would die
I've wondered where the time went
I've asked a lot of whys
Even with people around me
I've felt alone inside
Even through words of comfort,
My heartache couldn't hide,
I thought—I may be dreaming
I'd wake and find you here,
This can't be happening
While shedding another tear.
The day you were laid to rest
My heart shattered again,
I wondered if the pain would genuinely ever end.
It's hard to be without you,
At times the days seem long,
Sometimes I just sit crying,
Your death is so, so wrong.
I wish we'd had more time,
Before your life was done.
I hope you're resting peacefully,
My precious blessed son.

Written by: Renee Haley
June 2021

"What we
once enjoyed
and deeply loved
we can never lose,
for all that we love
deeply becomes
part of us."

—Helen Keller—

Birthday Prayers

The day before Austin's passing was my thirty-first birthday. Jack and the boys surprised me with balloons and streamers around the house. Jack bought me a birthday cake, so we enjoyed visiting while sitting around the dining room table eating dessert. Austin didn't care for cake, so he ate an apple instead.

We reminisced about the activities we enjoyed over the summer and how perfect it was to spend valuable time together. We had completed every item on Austin and Dalton's list of things to do.

Austin and Dalton brought me birthday cards and a few little "gifts" throughout the day, such as drawings or letters to make my birthday special. Jack gave me a beautiful watch, and I caught myself looking at it throughout the day, admiring how beautiful it looked on my wrist. We had a great time celebrating as a family. Little did we know, time was of the essence.

That evening—at about 10:00 p.m., I prepared our boys for bed.

As Austin and I wound down the conversation, I helped him put on his red Spiderman pajamas and gave him a small drink of water. As we were about to say his prayers, he stopped me.

"Wait, Mama. I want to pray for Grandpa, and I want to pray for you, too."

"Aww. Really? That's so sweet. I usually pray for you, but this time you're gonna pray for *me*?"

It surprised me at first, but I didn't have to think too hard to realize why he wanted to pray for us. My dad had suffered a stroke a few weeks prior and had lost sixty percent use of his arm; his entire right side was weak. He also battled Hepatitis C from a blood transfusion after he almost died from an oil rig accident in 1981.

I knew why he wanted to pray for me, too—I struggled with physical problems due to two previous miscarriages. We were unable to have more children for a year after the last miscarriage, and with the doctor's advice, we had scheduled a hysterectomy.

Austin said, "I am going to pray God heals your body, so we can have another baby in our home. I wish I could pick out the baby." His words hit me hard; I got goosebumps on my arms when he said them.

Jack and I taught him to believe with faith when he prayed, even though this prayer seemed impossible. "Son, pray and tell God what you want the new baby to be. Maybe He will answer your prayers in that way."

"Mama, would you want a boy or girl?"

"Hmmm . . . I'm not sure." I paused for a few seconds to consider his question. "I have you and Dalton already, so it would be amazing to have a little girl in our family, but I want whatever God wants, of course."

He acknowledged what I said in agreement. "But, Mama, I love my baby brother *so* much. It would be neat to have another little brother again, too. Don't you think?"

"Yeah, I would *love* to have another boy—especially if he is as wonderful as you and Dalton. I love you both so much." I snuggled my face close to his and covered his cheek with kisses.

After giving me several kisses in return, he looked into my eyes and asked another question. "What would you want the baby to look like?"

The question made me giggle. "You are asking tough questions, Son." I lapsed into silence for a few more seconds as I pondered. "You and Dalton look like your daddy, and I would love to have a baby who looks like me. Maybe with blonde hair like mine." I grinned at the thought.

Austin, a detail-oriented boy, appeared to be taking notes in his mind, not missing a single piece of information.

"But, Austin, you are as handsome and sweet as can be. I would love it if the baby looked like you." He sank his head lower into his pillow and glanced in the other direction. Even though his cheeks blushed, I could tell he liked the compliment.

It must've embarrassed him, though, because he switched topics. "I want to pray for Grandpa while you are in my room, but I want to pray for you after you leave." I thought it was a strange request since he had never asked me to leave the room.

"Umm, ok. Why can't I stay and hear the prayer about me? I want to hear your sweet prayer. Remember, I heard your prayer yesterday while you were sitting in my recliner. I overheard you saying the most precious prayer, repeating over and over again, 'I love you, God. I love you, Jesus . . .'"

"Yeah, I remember, Mama. God and Jesus love me a lot."

I couldn't help but have tears in my eyes hearing those words. It's so true.

Last night, when I overheard him saying those words I told him, "Austin that was such a beautiful prayer. God and Jesus love to hear you talk to them like that."

He got slightly embarrassed, and he told me he didn't know I could hear him. A couple of minutes later, he said, "Mama, I have a question. I have God in my heart and I have Jesus in my heart, but when am I going to have the Holy Spirit in my heart?"

"Well, that prayer was from your heart, Son," I replied. "Continue praying just like that. God, Jesus, and the Holy Spirit hear your prayers."

"So, Austin, you told me I can stay and hear the prayer about Grandpa, but can I, please, stay and hear the prayer about me, too?"

"No, Mama, sorry. You can't stay this time."

"Hmm . . . Ok, Son. I don't understand why I can't stay and hear it, but I will leave after your prayer for Grandpa. I'm just glad you're praying."

"Ok, Mama. I wish you could stay, too."

He closed his big brown eyes and began his prayers. I followed his lead and bowed my head, too. "God, please heal Grandpa in *one* day. Heal his body completely. He is weak and has Hepatitis C. He is so sick, but I know you can heal him, so please do it. In Jesus's name. Amen."

After his prayer, I told him how beautiful it was, but I was curious about something. "Why did you ask God to heal Grandpa in *one* day rather than right now?" With a surprised look, I could tell by his eyes he wondered *why*, himself.

"I don't know. I don't know why." He slipped into deep contemplation.

"Well, Son, I'll believe with you that Grandpa receives his healing. He needs healing. He's been sick way too long."

We gave each other a hug and a kiss as I tucked him into his blankets and spread his favorite bear blanket over him, so he could rub it between his fingers as he always did. I stood in the doorway of his room for a few more seconds to look at his handsome smile one more time.

"I love you!" I called as I stepped out of the room.

"I love you more!" he replied.

"Noooo—I love you more—all the way to Heaven and back!"

He giggled. "I love you more than that!"

We went back and forth a few more times before he reminded me he needed to finish his prayers for our new babies, so I flipped the light switch off. Shutting the door behind me, I heard his sweet voice saying, "I love you more, Mama. I love you too, too much."

As I walked the hallway toward Dalton's room, a smile curled at the edges of my lips. *That's a lot of love.*

In Dalton's room, we engaged in our evening snuggle time. My children had kind hearts, and I was blessed to be a mama to them both.

The nightly routine was the most precious moment I shared with my children because we always talked about our day, loved one another, and I got a few extra cuddles and hugs before going to bed myself.

Little did I know, though, it would be the last night I would fluff Austin's pillow, tuck him under his blankets, and kiss his cheek goodnight.

"Grief is like the ocean;
It comes on waves ebbing, and flowing.
Sometimes the water is calm,
And sometimes it is overwhelming.
All we can do is learn to swim."

—Vicki Harrison—

No, Bubba, Don't Go!

The day following the tragedy was beyond what any of us could bear. Before the accident, the morning ritual always included Austin entering Dalton's bedroom, making sure he did not startle his sleeping brother. He lay beside him on the bed, caressing and rubbing his little face.

Each morning when Dalton awoke, Austin was there to help pour Dalton's cereal. After breakfast, they would snuggle on the couch under Austin's favorite bear blanket to watch movies until Mama and Daddy awoke.

This day—the day after the tragedy—was painfully quiet, and our routine was no longer the same. Almost three years old, Dalton woke up that morning but didn't find his bubba next to him. Instead, he sensed something was wrong, and his daddy was waiting for him to awake.

He grabbed his daddy's hand. "Daddy, where is Bubba? Is he going to be okay?"

Fighting back the tears, Jack led him to me to answer the question. Jack stood behind Dalton with his hands on his little shoulders as I pondered how to give our child the worst news of our lives.

How do I say it? What words should I say? He loved his bubba so much. I don't want to do this! This is so unfair!

I stooped to my trembling knees and took him into my arms as tears streamed. I stared straight into his questioning green eyes. "Dalton, Baby, what I am about to say to you is so hard for Mama to explain. It makes me sad."

I swallowed hard and braced myself for the most emotional words my lips would ever mutter. "Your bubba, Austin . . . will not be able to . . . live here anymore. He went to . . . Heaven last night."

I broke when I said those last words, but I needed to be sure he understood, so I continued through my tears. "Austin can't come back to live here again, *but* we can go see him in Heaven someday."

I spoke as simply as possible, so he could understand. But, the words must have been too much for his little mind to bear. The words were too complex for *my* mind to comprehend. He propelled himself out of my arms with a scream that broke my heart. "No! No! Why? I don't want Bubba to go! I need him!"

His words, which mimicked the thoughts in my own mind, pierced my heart. *We all need Austin, and he should still be here with us! This is so unfair.*

The intensity of the pain in his voice was etched on his face and dropped me to the floor. I wept without taking a moment to breathe. *How can I help my baby? I can't even help myself—much less my baby boy.*

Somehow, I found the strength to force myself up. I had to because Dalton needed me.

After Jack hugged him, I lifted him into my arms, lowered into the recliner, and held him. I didn't want him to go through this pain.

The creaking of the recliner pounded in my ears, but otherwise, it was quiet. Dalton stared at the wall with such deep hurt. How long I held him, I can't say.

As I wept, tears streaked my cheeks and came to rest upon his little head. Still, neither of us moved.

Jack cried in the recliner next to us—often kneeling on the floor by Dalton and me, sweeping us both into his arms. We were now a broken family.

I now understood the saying, "silence is deafening." There wasn't a single movement in the room. No sounds of children laughing and playing. How could we live like this? Life was *forever* changed.

Oh, how our hearts shattered. How would we make it through this? Especially poor Dalton, who played with Austin every minute of the day? Helping him through this horrible agony of losing his brother felt like an impossible task. I love Dalton very much, and to see him so heartbroken was more than this mom's heart could bear.

I watched through the day as Dalton played with their toys, remembering the many times he and Austin shared them. He played make-believe as he had done with Austin, but no one played Austin's role anymore. I could tell playtime wasn't the same for him, and it broke my heart. Shattered it, to be honest. We all missed his brother's laughter and his high-pitched squeal when Dalton suggested a game. "That's a great idea, little brother."

I missed those times with Austin, the moments of sitting and talking, feeling his cheek next to mine while he spoke the words every mom loves to hear.

"I love you, Mama."

I'll never forget the way he felt in my arms and his sweet, tender voice.

That evening, Jack and I went to Austin's room in search of memories of him. We looked for drawings or fingerprints, anything and everything that was a part of him. We wanted to see it, touch it, and breathe it in.

When Jack lifted Austin's pillow, he found the core of an apple. Austin had never hidden one under his pillow before, but this time we were so glad he did. We stared at Austin's teeth marks. I looked at such a simple object with complete awe because soon I knew "time" would erase all traces of him from our home, and such a complex knowledge settled on my chest like a brick wall or like a hundred-pound weight.

I didn't want Austin to disappear from our family. The thought terrified me. Little by little, his memory would dissolve from our home.

Gone were the sounds of two sets of footsteps as Austin chased his little brother from one end of the house to the other. No more clicking of the orange play swords. No more sounds of the blissful life we knew before.

Tragedy

Dalton saw his brother fall to the dock the day before, on August 3, 2007. Again, I wondered how I would help Dalton through the atrocity he had witnessed.

"Mama, I looked at Austin, and he fell. My eyes did it. I made Austin die," Dalton told me. How could I help him through the torture of Austin being gone forever when I couldn't reconcile it for myself?

There was no way I could've prepared myself or my family for such a traumatic situation. On the days when it seemed all my strength was gone, I collapsed on the couch or my bed while anger, hurt, pain, and sorrow overwhelmed my heart and mind. Sometimes I vented my anger to God, and sometimes I couldn't speak a single word. I knew he understood my feelings, but still, the constant refrain of '*Why did this have to happen? Why, God?*' filled my mind.

At times, I would cry so hard I wasn't sure my prayers made sense. "God, help us. You see the hurt we are going through. Dalton misses his brother beyond words. Please help him, Lord. Give him peace and fill the hole in his heart with your love every day."

Many times, as Dalton thought about Austin, devastating loneliness filled his heart.

We all were angry and lost. Losing Austin was earth-shattering and forever altered our lives. The grief was so intense, so visceral.

I couldn't breathe at times due to grief, and I gasped for air to be able to live into the next moment. My heart ached so much it felt like it could explode from my chest. The depression and emotional exhaustion were challenging. My family and I needed help.

In the days following the shooting, our emotions hit with a vengeance. Fear. *Boom!* Anger. *Boom!* Sadness. *Boom!* Guilt. *Boom!*

Grief overwhelmed my mind, and the shots from the gun echoed through my thoughts minute after minute, moment after moment. The sounds of that day would not leave me. The *BOOM, BOOM* from the gunshots replayed daily in my mind.

My fists clenched tight as I struggled to deal with the idea that police officers took my son away from me.

One day, when I glanced at the watch Jack gave me for my birthday, I thought with indignation, *Time with Austin has been stolen away from me . . . precious time!* Why?

I was furious at the police officers—all three at the neighbor's house that day. What were they thinking? They shot their .357 pistol at my baby's head?

Rational thought told me they didn't *intentionally* shoot him—they couldn't see him directly—but it was a straight shot from where they stood to the pond—the place where my precious son fished and spent time with his grandpa, Papa Jim, and his brother, Dalton.

My heart pounded as our family gathered all the information about how Austin's death occurred. I thought back to the small town of Noble where we lived and how I grew up here.

The city of Noble is a 5A school district, so it is not a "tiny town," although it has a definite "small-town" feel since I know almost everyone who lives here.

I began school in Noble as a student in the second grade and eventually graduated from Noble High School in 1994. In 1998, I became a middle-school teacher in the school I attended as a child. Despite the traumas we've survived, I love Noble and everything about it.

Tragedy

The shooting should never have happened. First, it explicitly violated the law because there was no imminent threat when they shot inside city limits. Second, our house was within city limits requiring specific protocols to be followed to mitigate these types of tragedies.

If the weapon had been pointed to the northeast, it would have been pointed toward the high school and a housing addition. If the weapon pointed north, my house would have been in line with the trajectory. If they pointed it south, there's another housing addition. There was no "safe direction" the firearm could have pointed that day from that backyard.

To this day, I can't believe they shot their gun when the situation involved no imminent danger. The officers *thought* it was a venomous snake. A copperhead, I suppose, but it wasn't. Later, we found out it was a non-venomous black rat snake stuck in a birdhouse because its belly had become too enlarged from eating the eggs whole and couldn't dislodge. When snakes eat eggs, they dislodge their jaws to swallow the eggs whole, and then the eggs get stuck in their belly.

At the time of the shooting, the police officers were on a slight incline in the back of our neighbor's house, facing our pond. My son and the family were down a small embankment leading to the pond where they stood on a wooden fishing dock 510 feet to their east—about 300 feet further east than Jack's shop.

If the bullet had not hit my son, it could have been anybody in another housing addition on the other side of Austin, about two or three hundred yards away.

A few trees lined the rural plot of land, but my parents' twenty acres of property, on which the pond sat, was not "forest-filled" with trees blocking their view from my son. Instead, only a few bushes and thin trees blocked them from seeing my family on the dock.

We were in line with the officer's pistol, and they should never have fired those two fatal shots.

They should have seen my husband's bright red and white shop almost directly in front of them—the place my husband stood when the shots exploded. Couldn't they hear his music playing? Because *I* could. The police were closer to Jack than I was. So how could they not hear the music?

But, the shots were fired mere seconds apart from each other, and the second bullet hit my son.

Oh, my son—it can't be my little boy. The police officers—those tasked with serving and protecting killed my son with their gross negligence.

They shouldn't have shot—they were professionally trained and obligated to ensure they had an appropriate "backdrop," a known and explicitly safe trajectory of the shot bullets. So, there was no reason for shooting when they could have used other methods of removing the snake, such as hedge clippers, a rake, or a hoe. All three were lying at the police officers' feet.

In the developing investigative reports, the police officers said they had a backdrop, and it was a tree.

For whatever reason, though, they not only shot their gun, but they also *missed the snake and the nearly two-foot round tree in front of them by four feet.* Instead, the bullet came to a screeching halt when it barreled into my son's head.

The agony and pain tormenting my thoughts were more than this mama could bear, and to say I was angry was an understatement.

Tragedy

In some ways, it was easy to blame myself as I tried in vain to make sense of it all. There were so many variables that could have altered the trajectory of events that day, and Austin would still be in my arms where he belongs.

Why couldn't we have played on the swing set for a few more minutes before the boys left for the pond? They were only at the pond for *five* minutes. Why, why, why, didn't I say something to the neighbors whom I later realized were police officers when I heard their muffled voices behind our house talking about a snake . . . a fire . . . a hole? In retrospect, my intuition told me something was wrong. I felt it, but I shrugged it off as just a snake that needed to be removed. Should I have known danger was coming?

If I had spoken up and warned them that people were at the pond, is it possible they would never have shot their gun that day? But, I didn't know until it was too late that police officers shot their pistol behind the brush with only a few narrow trees separating them from my son.

Noble, Oklahoma, had a record amount of rainfall during the summer of 2007, so the dock where my son stood at the time floated higher than usual. If it hadn't rained so much and raised the dock, would my son still be alive?

Why couldn't my son have knelt to feed the fish rather than stand?

Why didn't you stop this from happening to us, God? I shook and trembled as the thoughts rampaged through my mind. *One little thing could have changed everything.*

"Blessed are those who mourn, for they will be comforted."

—Matthew 5:4—

The Dreaded Arrangements

Jack and I didn't feel like making funeral arrangements; we were in anguish. My mind wasn't working, and Jack's was as overwhelmed as mine. We had several questions to answer, however, so we pressed ahead. The excellent staff at the funeral home, who helped us the best they could, needed more information for Austin's death certificate. They also wanted to know whether we wanted an open or closed casket, what date we wanted to hold the funeral, what time we wanted it to be. The list went on and on.

My parents kept Dalton for us, so we could make the dreaded arrangements.

We had difficulty deciding which photos to include and what

words to write in my son's obituary. I took my seat in front of the computer and typed the obituary myself, with Jack helping to phrase it correctly. Even now, I don't know how Jack and I got through it all without a complete emotional breakdown.

The funeral home director took us to a room filled with caskets, each featuring various colors and designs. My mind whirled at what was required of me; I could barely stand without collapsing.

"I can't choose a casket," I told Jack. "I just shopped for his school clothes and classroom supplies." Somehow, with Jack's help, we made every decision required of us and left the funeral home, so they could finish preparations. We headed to my parents' home to pick up Dalton.

Tick. Tick. Tick. Mom and Dad's house was so quiet that I could hear the second hand of the grandfather clock as we opened the front door to Mom and Dad's house to pick up Dalton. In the living room, dimly lit that night by one small lamp in the corner, my dad cuddled Dalton to his chest. Mom was next to them in her nearby recliner.

There was a heavy pause as we entered. None of us knew what to say. Life was different.

"Dalton has been sitting in his lap for hours," Mom finally said.

"I'm glad he's been holding him close," I whispered. "I know they both need comfort. We all do."

Dalton didn't move an inch when we first sat on the couch on the other side of the room, but when my mom mentioned her candy box in the kitchen, he leaped down from my dad's lap and ran off into the kitchen for a sweet treat.

I shifted on the couch and imagined Austin running into the kitchen with his little brother, but he wasn't there. Instead, Dalton came back to the couch, sat on my lap, and we all discussed details of the upcoming funeral. About ten or fifteen minutes of that was all we could handle. Then, Jack, Dalton, and I left to go back to our house next door.

I didn't sleep that night. Instead, I lay in my bed and stared at the ceiling, glancing several times at my alarm clock to see how much time had passed. One a.m. Two. Three.

The next day, we cried as we trudged up the steps to the front door of the funeral home. Another impossible task loomed before us: view my son's body for the first time. Jack was by my side, as we made our way to the room which—impossibly—held our son. I dreaded walking to the casket. From the hallway, I could see it. It was so small.

How could this be? *My baby!* I took a few deep breaths before inching forward. Jack and I held each other for support, both physical and emotional, and my heart tensed up as I felt Jack's hand trembling in mine.

Why? Why were we saying goodbye when Austin's life had just begun?

The funeral home perfectly covered the wound on Austin's head with light make-up, making it possible for us to have an open casket at the viewing. I was so glad to see his little face, but I couldn't take the overwhelming burden on my heart.

Happy memories flooded my mind one by one: holding his hand, walking him through parks, snuggling him in my lap while reading books, laughing and running around the yard with him, enjoying time in the water sprinkler in the backyard, dressing him in a tuxedo for his five-year-old pictures.

Now, here he lay lifeless—in the same tuxedo, I used for those memorable photos.

My mind couldn't accept the immensity of life with Austin being gone. I couldn't remain on my feet. The overpowering grief slapped me to the floor, and there I lay on my back, weeping.

I demanded answers from God. "I don't understand why you had to take him so soon. I need him with *me*, but he can't come back, and I know that. Since he can't come back to *me*, will you at least bring me closer to *you*, God? Allow me to sit in your lap so I can feel close to Austin once again."

As soon as I finished those words, I sensed God lifting me up, setting me onto His lap, and wrapping His arms of comfort around me. I was exhausted and weary. "Oh God, help me," I cried aloud.

My husband and I prayed and cried over Austin in that funeral home for what seemed like hours. At one point, Jack leaned over Austin and talked to him, pleading that he would somehow hear from Heaven. Then Jack turned to me and said, "You aren't going to believe this, but I just heard Austin's voice say, 'Daddy.' I know that sounds crazy, but with a voice full of laughter, Austin said, 'I'm not in there; I'm up here.'"

I believed my husband. It seemed unusual, but the look on Jack's face told me it was true.

Then Jack said aloud to our son, "Austin, go to God and ask him to send us a message from you." He was desperate to hear from our little boy. We were both willing to say or do anything to hear from God or Austin. It was a lonesome time. An unimaginable ache from head to toe.

A few hours later, we left the funeral home and returned to my parents', where all the family members had gathered. We tried our best to eat a few bites of food in the large family room, but I felt cold and got up to retrieve a throw blanket from their linen closet.

I grabbed the first blanket I encountered. When I unfolded it, I noticed there was writing stitched into it. It was a blanket we gave to my dad some years ago for Father's Day. It had Austin's favorite verse on it, Jeremiah 17:7: "Blessed is the man, who trusts in the Lord, whose confidence is in Him."

I went back to the family room and showed everybody what I'd found. It felt as though Austin was speaking to me. Immediate chills ran down my spine. How could I reach into the linen closet and pull out a random throw blanket that contained Austin's favorite verse? As I read the words to myself, I could hear Austin's high-pitched voice reciting the scripture.

I unfolded the blanket a bit further and couldn't believe my eyes. In my heart, I knew it was a message given to Jack from Austin. Without a doubt, I knew my son had gone to our Father in Heaven and been granted permission to send Jack this special gift. I felt Austin speaking into my soul that day, and it brought me joy I hadn't felt in days.

Jack wept as he read a poem entitled "Dad," penned by T. Tilley, which was stitched into the throw blanket:

Dad
My dad is strong in character.
When times may test his faith, he stays
Steadfast and sturdy, trusting in God's grace.

My dad is wise and caring,
Strong, but gentle, too; and there's
Nothing like God's blessing of an earthly father, you.

After Jack read those words, we stood in the middle of the family room, hugged each other for a long time, and wept together. Our hearts were broken, but it seemed the throw blanket was a sweet message from Heaven, and it made us feel close to Austin once again. This sweet sign gave us hope that we could make it through this terrible storm we had brewing in our family.

When we returned to our seats to take a few last bites of our meal, a daunting task for grieving parents, I draped the throw blanket over my lap. Its heavy weight calmed my nerves, and I couldn't help but rub my fingers across the stitched verse that comforted my heart.

That evening, Dalton and I rode in my mom's car, during which Mom and I discussed the ordeal of making funeral plans for Austin. It was so surreal to have to make decisions such as what songs to play for his service or what photos to use for the slideshow.

All the decisions exhausted my mind. My oldest son would never be in my arms again. It couldn't be *the end* of what was only the *beginning* of his short life.

We headed toward the pond to piece together the nightmare from August 3. We couldn't sort out how it happened.

I sat in the backseat with Dalton, who stared out the window in silence and deep contemplation. When the fishing dock came into view, I wrapped my arm around him and pulled him close to me; I could see his mind drifting away to what happened only two days earlier, and I wanted to give him support.

"Son, are you alright?" I asked; though, I knew he wasn't. None of us were *alright* and would never be again.

He didn't reply with words at first. Instead, he lifted his hands in front of him and while locking eyes with me, made a circle with his tiny hands.

"Son, what are you doing? What is that?" I asked.

From the front seat of the parked car, my mom watched the scene unfold through the rearview mirror with complete attention.

Dalton tapped his fingers together, showed us the ball shape, and spoke these words,

"Sun. Sun." He stared into the round shape his hands made. He was serious about getting our attention, and he wanted to communicate something significant, but we didn't understand what it was. He stared out the side window in the direction of the dock.

"Dalton . . . Baby, did you see something?"

"Uh-huh."

"What did you see?"

We both looked at him with intensity as his next words seemed to be important to him.

Now, rather than making a circle with his hands, he brought his arms over his head in a sweeping gesture, forming a huge circle.

"Big! Big sun! Jesus came down and got Bubba!" He extended his hand toward me with his palm facing up and said, "Like this. He did this to Bubba."

His words shocked me.

Is my little son telling me he saw Jesus come and take Austin by the hand? How did he see that? Did he have a vision? It had to be a vision!

I didn't want to interrupt his thoughts, but I *had* to know what Austin did next. I needed to know every detail Dalton saw. I pleaded, "What did Austin do when Jesus held out his hand to him?"

Dalton reached his hand toward me and turned his palm down. "Bubba did this." Dalton turned his hand downward and put it into his other hand.

He looked through the side window toward the pond before continuing. "Jesus picked Bubba up. Bubba sang 'Jesus Loves Me' to Jesus. It made Jesus smile. He gave Jesus a *big* hug and kiss on the cheek. Jesus took Austin up, up, up."

Dalton pointed his finger higher and higher with each word he spoke.

"I told him, 'Stop, Bubba. Come back, Bubba!' But Bubba said, 'I can't come back, little brother. I'm going to Heaven, but meet me there someday!'"

The expression on Dalton's face was peaceful and determined. I had no doubt he would see Austin again.

Dalton's vision of Jesus taking Austin to Heaven was the most amazing thing I had ever heard. The vision combined with the special moment with the blanket, I believe, was foundational to the beginning of our family's emotional healing.

These words from Dalton the day after his brother passed away proved to be a sentiment that helped the family and me on more than one occasion. Rather than remembering the death, our family had something more peaceful to dwell on—Austin in the arms of Jesus! Our fears began to diminish, knowing Austin was safe and not in pain.

Even though we had good things to dwell on, such as the vision, the reality of living life without my son was daunting.

That night, I lay across my bed feeling intolerable grief without Austin. Yes, he was in Heaven. Dalton had seen him with Jesus. But that didn't heal the hole his loss left in my heart. Because of the intense pain, I turned onto my stomach, sank my face deep into my pillow, and sobbed. *How am I supposed to go on? He was my sweet boy. How do I continue living life?*

I turned my head to gaze at the Bible on the nightstand next to me. *Where should I turn in this time of darkness? How should I feel right now? I am so angry with the police officers. How will I ever forgive them? And should I even try? They killed my son—my son!*

Dalton's words about seeing Jesus rushed through my mind. *I saw Jesus pick up Austin.* I didn't have answers to my many questions; I couldn't think about anything at that moment. I was too weak. The vision God gave to Dalton, however, brought a sense of calmness to my mind. I was too weary to even think about blaming God. I needed Him more than I had ever needed Him before. I picked up my Bible and pulled on the zipper with trembling fingers.

I intended to read it. I wanted to, but I couldn't see the words on the pages through the blur of tears. Instead, I lay the open Bible across my chest, reliant on God to provide the strength I would need to make it through the rest of my life.

I was beyond distraught, and I wept aloud, *"Why, God, why did you have to take my son?"* I had no idea how to prepare for the dark days ahead.

"Grief, I've learned, is really just love. It's all the love you want to give, but cannot. All that unspent love gathers up in the corners of your eyes, the lump in your throat, and in that hollow part of your chest. Grief is just love with no place to go."

—Jamie Anderson—

News Media Calling

Three days after Austin passed, I woke up with profuse sweat drenching my body from head to toe. My heart raced. My head pounded, and it took a few more seconds to shake the feeling and realize it wasn't real. Instead, it was another horrible nightmare of police officers trying to kill my family.

I lay in bed panicking in an attempt to slow my breathing.

I stopped crying long enough to remember my plan for the day, so I got ready as fast as possible and headed to the police station.

I pulled off the road and into the police station's parking lot, then stepped out of the car and gazed up at the front door. It was the last place I wanted to be.

I opened the front door. My arms were weak with grief.

I didn't know the lady behind the glass, but she must have recognized me. She seemed shocked I was there. "Oh! Hi, Renee. What can we do for you?" Her face was melancholy, and it was difficult for her to make eye contact. She whispered, "I'm the one who took your 911 call."

I choked back tears, fears, and worry as the call flooded my mind.

I took a deep breath. "I wish we never had to talk that night. One thing could have changed everything," I replied.

"I know. Me too. I'm so sorry it happened."

"May I see the police chief for a few minutes?" I requested.

"Of course. I'll let him know you're here."

It was only a few seconds before he came to the front. He led me to his office, where he offered me to sit in a chair and visit. The last thing I wanted to do was have a detailed conversation. I tried to get what I needed and get out of there fast. I chose to stay standing, and so did he.

I asked my question fast. "Can I get a copy of any reports you have concerning my son, Austin Gabriel Haley?"

"What do you mean? We don't have any reports."

At that moment, I knew by his voice and the look on his face that he wasn't going to give me any information.

"I know police officers have records and maybe even video. I want anything . . . *anything* you have from August 3, 2007, when my son passed away." My voice was rising in anxiety.

"Renee, we don't have anything. No reports to give." He fumbled through a few papers in his file cabinet and his desk. I thought he was trying to find the documents, but not so.

"I know you have information from the night my son was shot.

There have to be documents or paperwork or *something*. If an officer reports a car crash, there is a ton of writing that must be done for their reports. My child died because of your department. I want records and anything else you have—now!"

"I'm sorry. We don't have a thing," the chief said. "I don't have anything to give you."

I felt like reaching up and shaking his shoulders like I did the police officer in our front yard when Austin passed away, but tears of frustration began to race down my face. I turned around and ran as fast as possible to get out of there.

I was out of his office and almost to the exit of the building when the lady behind the glass, the one who took my 911 call, whispered, "Ask for the radio control. They have to give you the radio control."

I barged back into the chief's office and demanded I get a radio control copy.

The chief didn't seem happy about it, but he told the 911 operator to make me a copy of the radio control and my 911 call.

I was thankful she helped me.

At least I left the department with *something*. After Austin's death, I needed anything and everything connected to my son. I needed to know every piece of information about how his terrible death occurred.

At home, our family was still running through the motions of what was *supposed* to be done. Whatever *that* is. Everything seemed to be a huge rush: answering the door for visitors, finding a place to stock the meals, meeting with the pastor about the upcoming service, and finalizing the funeral plans at the funeral home. Staying busy helped us cope, though.

We had no idea how busy life would become until the news of our son's death reached the news stations. The phone rang non-stop. When one phone call ended, the next call began.

Before we had a funeral for our precious five-year-old son, the media, internet, and newspapers published our family's story for the world to see. Worldwide news stations updated our story day after day, yet, I could never have imagined how closely our town, state, and nation watched as the days unfolded after the incident.

The world had never seen a situation like ours. A police officer, sworn to uphold the law, killed a child out of negligence because of a snake stuck in a birdhouse. It seemed every news channel around the world called us for interviews and wanted to know how we felt about it.

News reporters wanted to know if we would talk to them. We said, "Yes, we want the story released to the public, so we can get justice in this community. We don't want a cover-up."

When we heard the story told to the press by the police officers, I wondered if it was the same event we experienced. I wondered if the place the police described was the same place we had lived since 1983. Instead, the police and the Oklahoma State Bureau of Investigation portrayed it as only a likely accident.

They portrayed the location as a remote area, but it isn't hidden. It's in between several housing additions and the high school. It isn't possible to point a long-range weapon such as a .357 magnum in any direction without pointing it toward a school or a house. They reported using a big tree as a backdrop for the shot.

Tragedy

We cut down the grass and weeds between the birdhouse where the shot was fired and the pond to prove what happened.

We proved by using a transit; they missed the two-foot tree by four feet. They said the bullet was a ricochet, so we pulled a string from the birdhouse to the pond and showed a straight shot from the birdhouse to the dock where Austin stood that day.

Reporters were all over our property and agreed with our findings. The shot was fired in violation of ordinances prohibiting firearms shooting within the city limits. The fired attempt was reckless.

We thanked the many reporters in our area and around the world. Not motivated by revenge, we believed there should be accountability for the police officers' reckless actions.

Jack and I took several reporters to the pond to explain every aspect of the incident. The information superhighway spread the news about a "little evangelist" in "small-town Oklahoma" killed by an irresponsible police officer who shot his gun at a harmless snake, missed the snake, and hit our son in the head.

I was surprised at the overwhelming lights that blinded me from the news media's video cameras. It was more than I could handle at times, and I covered my eyes with my hands to get a break from the continuous flashes. Having to tell the story, again and again, was difficult and heartbreaking. Still, we shared it so the public could hear *our* side of the story as we knew the chief of police was not sharing the whole truth to hide his officer's reckless and tragic decision.

Each walk to the pond made me feel so disoriented due to the intensity of my grief. As I walked with the different media reporters, I held onto trunks of trees to remain on my feet. Jack and I would take turns answering their many questions, so we could force ourselves to breathe. Grief made me feel discombobulated, and I often held my breath.

I stepped on the wooden dock with Jack. We stood in the middle, the fish splashing under our feet. The fish were trained to come up and eat fish food by the sound of our footsteps or maybe our voices.

Hundreds of blogs carried the story via the internet as the account of Austin's life went viral. Our story was shown in Japan and Turkey. In addition, we received e-mail messages from Europe, Asia, the Middle East, and many from North America.

There was a great outcry of disbelief from many in the community of Noble, most of whom were friends, providing support and comfort to our family. Their children played with our children on ball teams and were friends with our boys.

Each person we encountered from the media treated us with kindness, but it wasn't easy to tell Austin's story to so many strangers. As the television cameras and bright lights focused on us, we explained the tragic details of our son's passing.

More than once, Jack and I pointed the reporters to the northwest, to the brick house and the snake's location. Sometimes I was angry, and I would cry, but I wanted the world to hear how much our family loved Austin. Even though we struggled through our anger and tears, we relied upon God for comfort and peace.

That evening, Jack, my parents, and I assembled around the living room in front of the TV. It had been four days since Austin passed. Our interview with local news stations ended a few hours ago, and now it was broadcasted on the local five o'clock Fox News Station.

My heart skipped several beats when I saw Austin's photo on the TV screen. I wanted to run, but my eyes were glued. I needed to hear every word that included any part of Austin's life--even if it was how he left this world. I cringed as I heard the words. "On Monday, three Noble police officers were placed on administrative leave. The officers responded Friday evening to a report of a snake in a birdhouse, according to a statement released Monday by the Noble Police Chief."

As we watched ourselves being interviewed from the dock, tears fell from our eyes. We sat in silence and listened to each word being said. My own interview was the hardest for me to listen to. My sobs were in sync with that woman who was behind the screen, recounting the story moment by moment.

As soon as the three-minute news clip was finished about Austin's story, our family was about to reflect on our thoughts and feelings, but the next news clip caught our attention. We returned to silence.

"A dump truck ran over and killed a fourteen-year-old boy in Oklahoma City today at 2:00 p.m. Thomas Glenn was jogging when the dump truck backed over him. The Oklahoma Highway Patrol did an on-site inspection of the truck and determined it should have never been in use. Five of six of the brakes failed inspection."

During the story, I watched as if holding my breath. I could feel the pain of his parents. Another child—gone.

I turned to Jack. "We need to go visit his poor family. They must be devastated," I said without hesitation.

"Yeah, that's for sure. How can we get in touch?" Jack asked.

"I bet the news station could help," Dad mentioned.

I stood up from the couch, scrambled away, and called the news station. The kitchen was spinning, and I braced myself on the kitchen counter to prevent a fall. Grief affected my body and my mind. I tried to shake away the feeling. My vision was a blur, but my fingers fumbled across the keypad. I was able to retrieve the information needed from the helpful lady on the other side of the phone.

That night, we drove to see Fay and Byron Glenn, the parents of Thomas, the boy who passed. The news cameras were there, but my focus wasn't on them—not this time. I walked up the driveway to knock on their door. Jack held Dalton in his arms and walked by my side while my parents walked behind us. Mom had a casserole in her hands. Fay opened the door, and I reached out, not saying a word other than, "I'm so sorry," and hugged her for a long time. All of us took our turn to hug Thomas's mom. She welcomed us into their living room. Fay and Byron knew we were coming. I could tell because the chairs were arranged in a welcoming circle. Fay introduced us to Byron, and we hugged him, too.

We sat for an hour or more, sharing our grief together. We expressed sorrow and shared stories of our young boys. All of us were in disbelief, and we were overcome by grief.

Fay stood up from her chair and grabbed Thomas's football jersey that was laying on the kitchen counter. Her fingers slid over the jersey: "I'm in disbelief. I can't believe Thomas is gone." Then, she picked up her son's cap from a shelf and placed it on Dalton's head.

Tragedy

"I want your little son to have Thomas's cap." The hat fell over Dalton's young three-year-old ears. It was too big, but that didn't matter. Dalton smiled for one of the first times since Austin passed and said, "Thank you!" He took the cap off and moved his finger over the multi-colored designs on the front. He was proud of his new hat and mentioned Thomas's name each time he put it on.

There was an immediate connection with Thomas's family. Throughout the years, we continued with phone calls, e-mails, and going out to eat with the dear family.

"I think the hardest part of losing someone isn't having to say goodbye, but rather learning to live without them. Always trying to fill the void, the emptiness that's left inside your heart when they go."

—Unknown Author—

Ripples of Grief

It was here—the day we dreaded more than anything—the day of Austin's funeral. It had been five agonizing days since his passing, an eternity for a family who would give anything to hear his sweet voice just one more time.

I love you so much, Mama. Austin's words burned in my heart, but my ears longed to hear them again. The inexpressible ache in my soul caused ripples of grief I never knew were possible.

That morning as I stood in front of the mirror to apply my makeup, black clouds of mascara stained my cheeks, and my chin quivered as I added lipstick with a tremoring hand. I stared at the person in the mirror but couldn't recognize the reflection because the person I saw was angry, sad, and lonely.

Renee, go ahead—allow yourself to cry. You don't have to be strong. You loved your baby boy, so allow the tears to express your love for him.

I placed my head in my hands and wept until nothing was left to cry. After a while, the wave of grief passed. Finally, I slipped into my black velvet dress and braced myself for what was yet to come.

Jack and I couldn't decide whether to bring Dalton to the funeral since he was young, so we allowed him to make his own choice. Only he knew how much he could handle.

He stayed with a babysitter and his cousin, Cooper.

As we pulled into the driveway of the church we had attended for over twenty years, my mind was a dense fog of overwhelming grief. Yet, somehow, we exited the car and made our way into the building.

Family and friends met us with hugs and condolences, but the calamity within my heart made me shudder and wish I could hide from everything this day entailed.

Jack and I greeted others while holding each other for support.

At 11:00 a.m., the funeral home director announced it was time to begin the service. We would now do the impossible—say our final goodbyes.

The sanctuary overflowed, and many people attended by television in the church's former building. In total, over six hundred fifty people were in attendance.

As we approached the front, our friends stood out of respect for the family, and I was shocked at how many people wanted to be there for us. Jack and I walked hand in hand down the aisle under the watch of hundreds of pairs of eyes. I remember thinking, *we have these many friends who love us?*

My eyes darted to Austin's casket, draped with his favorite bear blanket when the family sat. Austin, our little perfectionist, would have liked how seamless it was.

To the right side of the casket, Austin's five-year-old tuxedo picture sat on a golden tripod. He was such a handsome boy.

As I stared at the photo, memories of Austin flooded my mind. I recalled the day he played on the slide in the mall with the cutest smile on his face.

He rode a steep water slide on another day and rushed to my side afterward. "Mama, that slide made my heart beep."

I remembered when he searched for tiny frogs around our house and told me, "There are *tons* of frogs!" When I asked him how many he saw, he said, "One."

How could I forget Christmas? When he opened his Christmas gifts, he squealed with excitement every year, "This is the best Christmas *ever!*"

I relished making all those memories with my baby, and now they have been cut indelibly short. Five years of memories. That's all I had—all I would ever have because there wouldn't be any more memories to make with him after today.

God, how am I going to make it? How can I do this? I don't want to live without Austin. These were the thoughts rumbling through my mind.

Jack and I gathered enough strength to speak at the funeral about our son and the love he showed to us and everyone else throughout his short life. We both mentioned several memories we had of our sweet boy. We decided to focus on the good things about Austin's life and not mention the police or how his death occurred.

When climbing to the platform to take my place behind the

podium and microphone, I felt dizzy and weak, but I tried to stand tall while giving a eulogy about our precious son. As a rule, standing tall isn't difficult for me because I'm 6'4". My entire family is very tall, too. But on this day, I wobbled and stood like a toddler holding onto the microphone, trying not to fall.

I glanced up at the crowd. I couldn't look at the closed casket, not now. As I approached the front, I heard the gasps and whispers, sputtering, "How can Renee do this? She's so strong."

I didn't feel strong. I fumbled with the cordless microphone while the crowd watched, crying. I knew I was going to drop it. My heart pulsed with panic, nervousness, and exhaustion. I hadn't slept much in several days. I didn't know if I would be able to express my thoughts in complete sentences, much less tell memorable stories.

Somehow, I choked back the tears long enough to sing Austin's favorite song, "Jesus Loves Me." Then, I recounted stories about him. He was my little "preacher" boy from the beginning to the end of his five years, and I felt blessed to be his mama.

Jack spoke so lovingly about our precious son. Austin looked like Jack, and he adored his daddy. They enjoyed attending swap meets together, playing sports in the yard, and wrestling on the living room floor. Jack did a great job reminiscing and telling others about our son's short life at the funeral.

My sister, Michelle, and Jack's sister, Barbara, did a fantastic job speaking about Austin. They shared their memories and told of Austin's impact on their lives, and other people's lives with his joy, happiness, and love for Jesus.

Pastor Dean, our children's pastor, had very kind words to say about Austin, including the moments he got at Austin's eye level and handed him the microphone to say his favorite verse each Sunday evening. Pastor Dean and Austin always had something in common: they loved superheroes. It didn't matter which one—Superman, Spider-man, Batman, or Bibleman. They were all Austin's favorites.

After watching two video slideshows of his life, we listened to Austin's favorite songs and watched a video of him in the car, singing his favorite song, "Jesus Loves Me."

As Pastor Steve gave the message at the end of our two-hour memorial service, he used an acronym for Austin's name to show the six points Austin would want people to know:

A—Always trust in the Lord (even when you don't understand)

U—Use your gifts and time wisely for the glory of God

S—Show and tell your family you love them every day

T—Thank God in everything

I—Invest yourself in others

N—Near (The coming of the Lord is near)

The message he spoke described Austin very well. The full service, in my opinion, was the perfect memorial for my baby boy.

As the service ended, and before his casket closed, I leaned over my son's body and wept inconsolable tears. The unbearable pain of closing that casket stabbed my heart until I thought I would no longer survive.

Somehow, Jack and I said our goodbyes to our precious baby boy, who will never be more than five years, nine months, and ten days old in our memories. We followed the pallbearers as they carried Austin's casket to the hearse. Tears flowed from our eyes, and we took a seat in the front of a limousine along with my parents and Jack's mom and headed to Noble Cemetery.

The Cleveland County Sheriff's Department led the funeral

procession for the seven-minute drive from the church to the cemetery. Even through the mental fog and a cloud of depression, I noticed more people than I could count who lined the highway with signs in hand, showing respect to our family with prayers and condolences. Several pulled their cars to the side of the road. They got out of their vehicle and held their hat over their heart. It meant so much to see such support and love from our community.

Once we arrived at Austin's final resting place, my sister picked up our young boys, Dalton and Cooper, from the babysitter and met us at the cemetery.

We listened to our pastor read a few more verses and give words of encouragement. After the service, Jack, Dalton, and I released blue balloons to Austin in Heaven, whispering, "We love you! We'll see you again someday." Dalton looked upward and blew Austin a kiss goodbye.

After the tragedy, I asked myself, *why did Austin continue having that recurring nightmare about the police taking him from us? Why? Why did he ask so many questions about Heaven two weeks before he passed away?* He must've known he was going to leave us. He had to have known. There was so much left to understand, and I'm not sure we'll *ever* have the answers.

On the first day of our last summer together, I sat down with Austin and asked for a wish list of what he would like to do before kinder-garten began. He gave me a list of about thirty items, including going fishing with Grandpa, taking Dalton to Perfect Swing, a family fun entertainment center, shopping with his grandma, aunt, and cousins, and spending time with his nanny and best friends. His list was so simple and loving toward the people he cherished.

One of the things he wanted to do was go to a nearby kids' pizza buffet and play area called Incredible Pizza. Then, in late July, he told me, "We have to go there soon because we have to finish the list. *I don't have much time left.*"

It seemed Austin knew this would be the last summer with us. *How did he know?*

Austin's little voice wouldn't leave my mind from our last day together. *Mama, this is going to be a very bad day!* Even though I tried my best to make it a perfect day by pushing him on the swing, digging tunnels in the sand, and going to the pond, his three wishes for that day, I couldn't stop it from being a *bad day*. How did he know it would be a horrible day?

Jack and I both returned to our jobs two weeks later. It wasn't enough time since the tragedy for either of us, but we needed normality in our lives. So I went back to teaching sixth-grade students in our small town of Noble while Jack returned to Tinker Air Force Base in Midwest City, Oklahoma, to inspect airplanes. Things were better for us emotionally while at work—but at home, grief slapped us in the face every time we walked through the front door.

On one harrowing day, I drove up to our driveway after school, and the grief not only slapped my face but charged at me full force.

I crawled out of the car, fell to my hands and knees on the sidewalk, and wept. I'm not sure how long I stayed on the cold, hard cement before I mustered enough strength to pull myself up and go into the house. Grief hurts!

My heart was crushed, and even as the days and months passed, I felt lost and alone. The pain was intense. At times, I couldn't function while completing the most mundane tasks. Brushing my teeth or combing my hair became an arduous job. Dinner in the oven, burnt. Water in the sink overflowed. The refrigerator door stood open. The laundry piled up to my knees. My clothes felt like someone else's clothes. My shoes. Were they even mine? And where was I going? Oh yes, school. Daycare. Home. Dinner. Dishes. TV. Bath for Dalton. Shower for me. Repeat. Somehow, I made it through each day. How? I don't know. Most days, I felt I could not go on. I couldn't move.

In the mornings after getting ready for school, I'd walk past Austin's bedroom door and realize he wasn't there for me to wake him for preschool. My knees would buckle, and I'd stare forlorn at his empty bed. My heart longed for him to be there.

Nothing and no one could ease my pain. I knew it wasn't possible, but I needed Austin back in his bed where he belonged.

God, please, help me! I cried over and over. But the pain didn't stop. Instead, it grew like a snowball rolling bigger and bigger down a hill that didn't end.

Tragedy

One night, Jack glanced into Austin's bedroom and noticed Austin's dirty laundry piled in the laundry basket. He lifted the superhero shirts to his nose, realizing his scent would soon dissipate and leave our home for good. Overcome with emotion, he lay across Austin's bed and wept.

From where I sat in the living room, I heard his weeping and went to Austin's room to see what was going on. I clutched Jack in my arms and cried with him. "Why, God? Why us?"

My emotions were all over the place. I was *up*, remembering the good times, and *down*, remembering his death. I felt intense anger toward the police officers and was fearful I might lose Dalton somehow. I felt lost, unsure of what I should do now, and I was sad that our life was changed forever.

How should I be feeling? I didn't know.

Grief was a never-ending roller coaster—full of ups and downs, highs and lows. I'll never forget how I prayed, "God, please give us something *good* to think about because my heart hurts too much from this pain."

<u>Letters to my Brother in Heaven:</u>

They say there is a reason
They say time will heal;
Neither time nor reason
Will change the way I feel.
Gone are the days
We used to share.
But in my heart
You are always there.
The gates of memories
Will never close:
I miss you more than
Anybody knows . . .
Love and miss you every day
Till we meet again
Always & Forever

—Unknown Author—

Dalton's Questions Begin

Every day that passed, I missed Austin more and more. We all did. Though attempting to figure out how to deal with my own grief, I knew I also needed to find it within myself to be present to help Dalton deal with his grief.

I didn't feel like doing anything most days, but I *forced* myself to crawl to the middle of the living room floor— to sit where Austin sat and play the same games Austin and Dalton played together. My husband did the same.

Our willingness to do this brought a little more happiness to Dalton's world and a little normality to his uprooted life. It also helped me to remember many of Austin's favorite games and toys.

I longed to see Austin and Dalton playing together again with

Transformers, pretending they were superheroes, running and chasing each other through the house, laughing in youthful playfulness, and riding in the little yellow battery-powered jeep in the backyard together. Anything they could get into, they did, and the silence of our little dynamic duo no longer existing was excruciating for all of us.

As a family, we often talked about Austin's death for a while, cried a bit, and got back around to playing again.

"Honey, what do we do now?" I asked Jack, desperate for answers. "What is the next step we take?"

I sat on the floor next to Dalton, helping him line up Austin's Hot Wheels Cars by color along the living room rug. Red in the first line. Orange in the second. Yellow in the third row. A Hot Wheels Garage Toy was on the floor between us, and occasionally, Dalton and I added another one in the different compartments, so we continued our car "business" together, one that Austin and Dalton co-managed a few days ago. Each compartment held different colors of cars.

"We're going to court." Jack replied, "We're gonna have to. The District Attorney heard about our case, and he called me this morning."

My heart skipped a beat. "What did he say?" The pitch of my voice was high, nervous.

"He said he's never heard of another case like ours. Ever."

"Yeah, I don't doubt that. So, are we going to get an attorney or what?"

"No, we can't. I asked, and they said we can't."

"What do you mean? We don't have a right to hire an attorney?"

"No, I guess not. When there is a criminal case against the state, the district attorney is the one who helps. That's what he told me on the phone. From what I understand, he is going to help us in court. The

District Attorney said he'll be our advocate, and your dad can be an intermediary attorney. I think that's what he said, anyway."

"What does that kind of an attorney do? Did you say, *intermediary*?"

"Yeah, from what I understand, your dad will discuss the details with the attorneys from both sides of the case and then explain it to us."

"Oh, okay. That makes sense. Sort of. But, all of this is so confusing. I don't know legalities—my dad does, but I don't."

"Neither do I. I guess we do the best we can, and hopefully, your dad can help us."

I watched as Dalton closed the garage door on the Hot Wheels toy to signify that business was "closed" for the day. I stood up, returning to my recliner next to Jack, slipping the throw blanket with Austin's favorite verse over my legs.

I looked over at Jack.

"My dad is grieving so much that I doubt he can concentrate on our case, but I know he will do what he can to help. At least we'll have the District Attorney to answer most of our questions."

"Yeah, both the District Attorney and his Assistant DA are supposed to help us figure out how to prepare for court. They'll be calling us and giving us more information soon."

There was no more talk of court. At least not that night.

The struggle was real, and there was so much to consider.

I glanced over at Dalton. His eyes were glossed over, and he seemed sad. I worried about our little boy's feelings so much, and I felt it was essential to be as transparent with my own feelings as possible. That way, if he ever needed a shoulder to cry on, he felt comfortable coming to me. At times, I told him, "I feel sad because Austin is not here with us anymore." Or "It made me feel angry when Austin was shot."

To which Dalton often responded, "Yeah, me too."

I knew Dalton was as miserable and angry as Jack and me.

How could he not be?

Still, I needed to assure that Dalton knew it was fine to have those feelings, and we welcomed him to speak with us about it anytime he needed.

On many occasions, he saw me crying while vacuuming the carpet or loading clothes in the washer, and he ran over and wrapped his little arms around my legs, giving me the most comforting words ever. "It's okay, Mama. I'm sad, too."

I bent down and wrapped my arms around him, pulled him into my lap, and gave him a long, heartfelt hug. It was a gesture that helped both of us. Despite his young age, I knew Dalton felt the same level of grief as his daddy and me. I knew our almost-three-year-old boy couldn't comprehend or articulate as much as us adults, but I knew he experienced the same feelings.

At times, the things he said or asked weren't easy to hear. Nevertheless, Jack and I encouraged him to talk to us about anything that crossed his mind.

He asked more difficult questions than I could ever count, and sometimes he asked the same questions often, but I didn't mind. I wanted him to understand everything that happened on that life-altering day.

"What was the blue thing Austin was laying on when they put him in the ambulance?" he asked one day.

"Baby, a gurney is a blue bed they lay people on when they go to the hospital in an ambulance," It made me cringe to recall the moment they loaded him into the emergency vehicle.

"Why was Austin so red when he fell on the dock? His arms were red, too."

As difficult as these types of questions were to answer, I replied with complete honesty. "It was blood on Austin's body, Honey. Do you remember when you fell and cut your leg? It bled a little, right? Well, when Austin got shot, it made him bleed, too."

As weeks and months passed, Dalton still remembered even the tiniest details of what happened on that harrowing day. He still spoke about his memories of his brother's deadly encounter.

As we dug in the sand one day, he said, "Mama, if I had a towel that day, I could have cleaned him off. He would have been fine."

With as much calm as I could muster, I explained to him there was nothing anybody could have done to help—not Daddy and Mama, not even Grandpa or Grandma could've helped him. I wanted to relieve him of any guilt he placed on himself. I knew he felt guilt about Austin's tragedy because I knew I did. I believe feeling guilty is an expected response after an immense tragedy.

The repetitive thought overwhelmed my mind. *If I had asked the neighbors if they needed help with the snake, it wouldn't have happened.*

Jack and I reassured Dalton that nothing from that day was his fault.

"Mama, why did Austin want to leave me and go to Heaven?" Dalton asked one day as I pushed him on the swing.

"Dalton, Bubba didn't *want* to leave you. He loved playing with you and being your big brother, but police officers made a bad, bad decision to shoot the gun. It was a terrible accident. They didn't mean to kill him, but they did."

One question always led to another, but it was fine because it was a three-year-old boy's way of processing his feelings.

After the incident, he became petrified of police officers and trembled whenever one was near. "Are the police officers going to shoot me? I'm scared of them," he told me several times.

Any time we or any of our family members saw a police officer, we experienced a fresh surge of anger, bitterness, and deep hurt. We all had this instant thought to run far away when we saw a police officer.

When I drove in the car and saw a police car moving in my direction, my palms would sweat as I gripped the steering wheel so hard my knuckles turned white. I had to remind myself to concentrate on my driving and breathing instead of the police car outside my window.

The fear we felt toward police officers was immense, and the feelings were beyond what I could ever explain.

There was a rage inside me that would never vanish. I couldn't help but feel anger toward *all* the police officers, and we were suspicious of every one of them. It did something to our subconscious minds.

As a family, we spoke with a psychologist, and she said we battled PTSD, Post-Traumatic Stress Disorder. We were often startled and frightened at loud noises or quick movements.

When I felt endangered or threatened, it was a quick flip of a light switch. There was no warning, and the reaction came fast. I broke out into a profuse sweat, my heart skipped beats, and I clenched every muscle in my body from head to toe.

Once I made sense of everything, my breathing would return to normal.

We were triggered by "men in blue" with guns on their hips and shiny badges. As soon as I saw one of them, my mind flashed back to that horrible moment, and I broke out in a dripping sweat. Nightmares plagued my mind with dreams of police officers coming to kill the rest of my family and me.

With each nightmare, I somehow got away from the officers chasing me, only to awaken at the last second in a panic, sitting straight up in bed and sobbing with sweat drenching me. My heart thumped so hard from anxiety I thought I would die.

It took a lot of prayers to conquer these thoughts because deep down I knew not all police officers had killed our little boy. Not *all* police officers would have made the same decision that terrible day.

When several months had passed after the funeral, I saw two police officers at a restaurant in our hometown. I knew I needed to do something when I saw the fear rising in my little boy's eyes.

Without Dalton's knowledge, and with great concern on my part, I approached the police officers and whispered to them about Dalton's fears—of all our fears.

Even though I trembled, I made myself do it, so I could somehow, someway help Dalton be free of his fears. Maybe, it would help me, too.

I asked the police officers if they would mind getting on his level to speak to him. I wanted to make sure he knew police officers were there to *help* him if ever needed. I didn't want him to struggle with the memory of his brother dying on the dock each time a police officer passed by him.

He needed peace, and I hoped those two police officers would help calm his mind.

When Dalton approached them, the two officers knelt, gave him a high-five, smiled, and spoke to him for several minutes. Who knew a simple gesture like a high-five could help alleviate many of his fears toward police officers? And, somehow, it helped me, too.

Not all police officers make wrong choices. Not all police officers are in the wrong. Jack and I knew this, but at times it was hard to remember when it was tangled with the emotional torture we felt.

The gesture of those two kind men gave Dalton one small moment to build back trust with police officers, but the journey was far from over.

I didn't want to be on this horrible journey of grief, despair, worry, fear, anxiety, and loss. It was so unfair! *Why do we have to go through this pain? Why me? Why my family?*

The incident with the two officers in the restaurant was a small step in the right direction, but how would we ever trust police officers again?

Fears overwhelmed my mind in the least expected moments.

In the weeks before Dalton was to begin Pre-K, I told him it was time to get his last set of shots before school started back again.

Dalton sank into the recliner, crying and shaking from head to toe.

His unexpected reaction stunned me, and it took me a few seconds to process.

He pushed me out of the recliner and stood to his feet. "Okay. Mama, can I get one last hug from you? I will miss you." Tears streamed down his cheeks.

"Son, why would you say that?" I said, shocked at such a statement. "We are only getting a sho—" I stopped, and it broke my heart to realize what he thought I meant. He thought he was about to get shot—like his big brother, Austin.

I knelt at eye level and reassured him he wasn't getting shot with a gun. I explained that a doctor would place a small needle with medicine in his skin.

He relaxed and felt better after the explanation, "Oh, okay. I'm going to be brave then."

From that time on, I made it a point to call them "immunizations" instead of shots.

The emotions he endured were tough for me to witness as a mother. Like all parents, I wanted to give my children a happy life, free of pain. It was the life I had dreamed of since my teenage years while dreaming of being a mother. All this trauma, however, was far from what I had wanted for Dalton in his young childhood.

It hurt my heart to see him going through such pain. We not only had to deal with the initial tragedy of losing Austin but also with other so-called tragedies that popped up after *the* tragedy—ripple effects from the initial loss.

My son's death was a calamity for our family, and the emotional pain was another issue to deal with. Anger, confusion, loneliness, and despair became unwanted feelings for us all.

The anguish and pain of losing Austin captivated my every thought. I had headaches so bad, it felt like someone hit me in the head with a sledgehammer. Other times, I was dizzy and out of breath, and the walls closed in on me.

Our faith was strong; our bodies were weak. Life was so different now, and I needed relief.

Even through the moments of despair, I wanted to feel Austin was with us by remembering him in special ways. Despite our grief, our family concocted many different ways to honor his life.

It helped us through the difficult times, but it also gave us something to keep our minds occupied.

Here are a few of the things we did with our family and the children who missed Austin as much as we did:

- Talked about our feelings and memories
- Remembered fun times together
- Answered the children's questions—even if it was two or three times in different ways to make sure they understood what happened
- Wrote letters to Austin, laminated and placed them on his headstone
- Picked out a toy or another item for the gravesite
- Drew pictures about what happened to Austin
- Attached notes to balloons and released them to Heaven,

asking the person who found the balloon to give our family a call.

**It surprised us when we received a call from a woman in San Antonio, Texas, on her birthday. She had received the balloon 450 miles away. The phone call brought us much comfort.

- Picked out toys or objects around the house that were special to Austin and placed them inside a curio cabinet for safekeeping
- Planted a tree with Dalton tasked to water it each morning
- Lit a candle on special days
- Made a memory box or scrapbook
- Wrote a story about Austin

I realized the struggles of life were apparent in the most unexpected ways after experiencing our traumatic event. My soul ached when I thought of the tragedy, so these things gave us a little good in our lives.

"Grief is the last act of love we can give to those we loved. Where there is deep grief, there was great love."

—Annette J. Dunlea—

My "Griefcase"

"Yes, we will meet with you," Jack spoke on the phone. "We'll see you in about an hour."

Before I knew it, we were in the car, heading to Oklahoma City.

The District Attorney and his assistant invited Jack and me along with my parents to his office, and that's when we let the District Attorney know we wanted to see jail time for the officers involved with our son's shooting—the one who shot the bullet and the supervisor who told him to shoot the bullet.

It didn't go as expected. I thought they would feel the same way, but their opinions were different. Very different.

"Here's a cup of water for you to drink," The DA told Jack. "Why don't you talk about it for a while and make your decision carefully? I don't know that jail time would be the answer in this case."

Jack spoke up. "We already *have* thought about it. Most people would want the officers to be in jail for *years* if this happened to their child. All we are asking for is at least thirty days to set a precedence for other cases like ours. We've already discussed it thoroughly between us. We don't have to *think* about it anymore."

The DA left the room for a few minutes. I'm not sure where he went.

Ten minutes later, he walked back in. "Hey, family. Did you have enough time to think about it some more? I'm sure you decided that jail time is *not* the best decision in this situation, right? We feel community service may be a better idea."

My mom spoke up to tell him otherwise. "Jack and Renee have told you how they feel. They want to see some days in jail. What do you not understand about that? If it were your child, wouldn't you want the person who shot the gun to sit behind bars for a while? It's only right—even though they're police officers. Those police officers should be treated just like everyone else who has done something so negligent. Remember, Austin was shot because of a snake. That's it! It was only a non-venomous black rat snake. The police broke the law!"

"Well, let us think about it and speak with the officers and their attorneys. We'll call and let you know what we've decided."

Tragedy

When back at home, the thoughts wouldn't leave me. What kind of boy would Austin grow up to be? I had anticipated watching him grow from a baby to one day graduating high school, college, and having a career. *What would his occupation be? Whom would he marry? What would my grandchildren be like?* The list went on and on. My dreams were crumpled. Nothing but ruins of *what could have been* filled my mind.

There were no more "What will he do next" scenarios—no more memories to make. It was so unfair his life had come to an end! At times, my heart couldn't take the throbbing stabs of pain.

Not long after the tragedy, as I loaded the dishes in the dishwasher, I noticed his little teeth marks on one of the plastic cups he had drank from, and I leaned over the kitchen counter, sobbing.

At other times, as my husband drove our car, out of habit, I'd reach my hand behind the front seat to hold Austin's hand before I remembered he wasn't there. His little fingers were no longer there to wrap around mine.

How do I do this? How do I go on? How do I cope? At times, I shuttered in fear, and other times, I was forlorn without having my sweet boy to embrace in my arms. *How can I ever smile again?*

The feeling was indescribable—my "griefcase" as I came to call it, was tattered, worn, and tarnished, and the weight of it almost broke me.

My griefcase was filled with anger, guilt, fear, and sadness, but our lives had to continue one way or another. I didn't know how, but I had to make it happen.

Guilt swept over me when I smiled or when I cleaned one of his fingerprints from the glass in our house. Fears ignited when I passed by police officers—even after speaking to them for Dalton's help.

The feeling of sadness after Austin's passing was constant. Anger was my dominant emotion when I thought of how negligent the police officers were. Everything could have been so different. Austin would still be here if the police officers had made other choices that day.

Yes, I was angry they shot the gun and killed our son. He still would have been here with us and playing sports—especially basketball (He never got the opportunity to play). He may have continued with football and baseball—who knows.

Even through my heartbreak, I tried to stay as busy as possible so I wouldn't sink deeper into depression. That's the last place I wanted to be. I couldn't let myself go there. *But, what can I do to help myself?*

My Griefcase was also filled with bitterness, anxiety, loneliness, shock, and helplessness beyond belief. Nothing or no one could ease my pain. I knew it wasn't possible, but I needed Austin back—with me.

Grief was painful, not only emotionally but also physically. My body ached as if the flu virus had attacked me from inside out. I couldn't sleep, and I didn't feel like taking a single bite of food to nourish my body. Part of me died with Austin that day, and my heart shattered like a broken mirror into hundreds of pieces. I would never be the same person I was before the tragedy.

The heartache and pain were a black cloud covering my every move. I didn't want to be carrying this "griefcase," but what else could I do? I had no choice in the matter.

I went through so many different emotions, I never knew how I would feel from day to day or even minute to minute.

I couldn't keep up with my evolving feelings, and on many days, I felt numb and sat in a dark room. I no longer knew what to feel or what was appropriate to say or do. Our family was weathering a major storm while enduring all the feelings in the griefcase. It was like a tornado that never stopped swirling, tossing me from here to there, but unlike natural tornadoes, this emotional tornado failed to cease. There was no way out. No way to escape.

In the living room, I glanced up at his picture on the wall. It was his smile I loved the most. I stared at his smile for a minute or two, even walking up to touch it, rubbing my fingers over his lips and teeth. How would we ever be happy again? Our family was so perfect, at least in my eyes, before the tragedy, and now, true happiness seemed so far away.

Questions haunted my mind. *How did Austin know he was going to die?* My husband and I both found it *so* unusual that Austin knew of his upcoming death. *How did he know?* It was such an odd, eerie thing for a little five-year-old boy to know he was going to die on that very day.

The nightmare would never be over. *Would we ever enjoy life again?*

A few other feelings I faced were confusion, forgetfulness, and disbelief. The list went on and on. My griefcase was packed with a plethora of sad thoughts and feelings.

Where do I turn? What do I do now? Who can help me?

I didn't have to carry the heavyweight alone, though, because Jack was beside me every step of the way. Also taking the journey with us were my parents, who taught me that God was my Restorer.

Weeks after the incident occurred, the prayers that Austin had prayed the night before passing away were answered because my dad's strength from his stroke returned.

There was a reason Austin prayed for Grandpa. Our boy may not have realized it, but my dad would need healing after the death of his grandson, and not just a physical one. Austin's prayer gave my dad comfort throughout the most challenging time in his life.

At times when I felt depressed, I took my Bible in my hands, closed my eyes, and prayed through my exhaustion, "God, you know how I feel right now. I can't go on. My world is shattered like broken glass. Lord, please speak to me through your Word. Somehow, someway, help me find strength."

I pled for God to open *His* griefcase in my heart. I knew *His* grief-case would be easier for my heart to handle. I needed His help and His strength, but it felt like my feet were mired in quicksand with no hope of being free again. I needed him to bring healing to my heart and ease the anger within my raging soul.

He must have heard my heart's cry because we received terrific news a month after Austin's death. I was expecting another baby. *What? Am I expecting a baby? How can this be? I had a hysterectomy scheduled and the doctors told me I wouldn't be able to have another child, but, God, You brought something good our way.*

We needed hope and joy, so He answered yet another of Austin's prayers. He already healed my dad's weakness from the stroke, and now, a new baby was on the way.

It was the first time Jack and I smiled in a month. The thought of another baby in our home and a child for Dalton to play with gave us something to look forward to.

The daunting silence would be broken. There would be a spirit of playfulness in our home once again.

October 24, 2007, almost three months after Austin passed, he would have turned six years old. It was difficult to know what to do for his birthday. I wanted to hear his laughter, run with him in the yard, give him gifts, and sing, "Happy Birthday." That's the way it should've been, but it wasn't the same anymore. So, what do grieving parents do? What are we *supposed* to do after the loss of a child? We were lost without answers, and it was an unexplainable void.

Jack and I decided to invite the community out to our house, and have a memorial for Austin. We invited family, Austin's friends and their families, and his football team. Our church family was also in attendance.

Earlier in the week, I ordered one hundred balloons. It almost wasn't enough. We were surprised that there were nearly one hundred people who knocked on our front door. We felt so much love and support from our family and friends.

It brought tears to my eyes when I noticed many of Austin's young friends were wearing matching memorial t-shirts. The gray shirts included Austin's first and last name, a camouflage football with Austin's football number 23, and Jeremiah 17:7 was written under the logo. The t-shirts were designed by some of our closest friends, and it was a surprise to our family.

All of the people who came to honor Austin for his birthday gathered in the front yard. The balloons were passed around to each person, and we walked together to the pond.

Our immediate family, our parents, and grandparents stood on the dock. My dad read a few verses in the Bible, including Austin's favorite, Jeremiah 17:7. My dad's voice shook, and he choked back tears. Standing on the dock was never going to be easy again, but for some reason, we were drawn to spending special moments there.

After my dad shared a few comforting verses, Jack's family sang uplifting songs, harmonizing with a heavenly sound. After reminiscing and telling a few stories of Austin, the crowd each released their balloon. The sky became a sea of colors, and I felt Austin would smile from Heaven if he could see us and the balloons. We all watched in silence until the balloons disappeared from sight.

We laid a three-ring binder on a nearby table, and our family and friends wrote their favorite memories of Austin. It is a keepsake we read through often. While our friends began visiting, I saw Austin's closest friends crying and wrapping their arms around each other in support. Jack and I knelt to give each one a comforting hug. They needed us, and we needed them. Oh, how special Austin's friends are to us.

By the end of the gathering, it was difficult to see each person leaving, but we were so thankful they shared Austin's sixth birthday—his first birthday in Heaven—with us.

"There are no quick fixes to grief.

No easy answers.

Every expression of grief

that wants to be felt

and honored and

given its space,

must be allowed . . .

in order to heal."

—Tom Zuba—

Battle in the Courtroom

On March 28, 2008, only eight months following our unimaginable tragedy, Jack and I walked into the courtroom for the legal hearing. Every seat was full. Only family and friends were allowed in the courtroom—no media or the public could be inside. Our family sat on the left as we faced the judge while both officers' families filled the right.

Jack and I took our seats as my face burned with anger and my fists clenched, waiting for my opportunity to speak face-to-face with the police officers who were responsible for my son's death. Judge Lucas allowed an unlimited number of family members to speak whatever was on their minds, and fourteen spoke.

As an attorney, my dad had tried cases for several years in front of

Judge Lucas, and they were friends. It surprised me that they allowed us to present our case inside his courtroom, but my dad was familiar with all judges in our central area of Oklahoma anyway, so it didn't matter. I was happy to see Judge Lucas as the presiding judge, though, because my dad thought well of him, and that was good enough for me.

I glanced at the notes I held in my lap with trembling fingers and noticed my pregnant stomach had grown. Due to my rising anxiety from the anticipation of the hearing, I could feel the baby quivering inside me. I rubbed my stomach and took deep steadying breaths to calm my nerves. My fears of losing this baby were overwhelming because I had battled two previous miscarriages. Every day, the cry of my heart was, *Please, God, don't let me lose another baby!*

A hush settled over the crowd as the judge walked from behind the back wall and took his seat and banged his gavel on the desk. He spoke with a voice of authority, which made us sense the seriousness of our case.

"In the matter of State of Oklahoma, the two police officers sitting before me today enter pleas of no contest."

A deep, angry gasp escaped my lips, and I turned to glare at the two men who stared straight ahead. *Those police officers are guilty! They should be admitting their guilt rather than allowing the court to decide.* I wanted to scream to anyone who would listen.

As the judge read through the evidence, I heard new information I never heard before that day.

Clips of statements the judge read stood out to me more than others. One of them was, "There was a call to the police station that came from Jack and Renee's next-door neighbor who discovered the snake (in another neighbor's birdhouse). The neighbors who owned the birdhouse were not present at the time."

What? So, the neighbor who made the call to the police station didn't own the birdhouse? It was in another neighbor's yard, and that neighbor wasn't even home at the time?

Later, the judge reviewed what the police officers did before the shot was fired. The judge read, "The supervisor walked toward the back of the neighbor's fence and yelled, 'fire in the hole' in the direction of the open field, and walked back toward the house. That's when the supervisor had ordered the rookie police officer to shoot, having graduated four months earlier from Council on Law Enforcement Education and Training, otherwise known as CLEET, a police officer training school in Oklahoma."

So, that's what I heard the police speaking about as I played in the sandbox with my boys. I only heard the words 'snake,' 'fire,' and 'hole,' but they must have been discussing the idea of yelling, "fire in the hole" before firing the gun.

I cringed as I remembered hearing those words right before I started the lawnmower. At the time, I had no idea what "fire in the hole" meant.

In the last few months of discussing it with my husband, he said he was familiar with the phrase due to the military. Jack said, "It means that an explosion is imminent." Now, how was *I* supposed to know it was a warning? I've never been in the military. The average person wouldn't know what it meant or what to do if they heard this. And did the officers expect us to know what this meant and to immediately take cover? If so, in what way did they expect people to take cover?

But, the thought caused me additional guilt. If I would've known, I could have yelled out to stop what was about to occur, or could I? The thought of being able to save Austin haunted me.

The judge discussed all the evidence and then called Jack to begin the testimonies.

Jack was direct and thorough as he addressed his thoughts. "My son, Austin Gabriel Haley, was a miracle child. The doctors said we couldn't have children, but not long after, Renee became pregnant with Austin. We counted him as our miracle, and that miracle was stripped away from me because of the negligence of these police officers. This hurt me, and it gave me a life sentence."

After that, Jack discussed the sentencing of the police officers. There were no other cases similar to ours in the nation that could be found in the law books, and my husband requested the police officers sit in jail for thirty days or more to have time to think of their negligence from that terrible day.

I thought about the number "thirty days." Our family discussed this number with my dad for the past month or two. In some ways, I wondered if we should have requested more, but it wasn't about the police officers sitting in jail or prison for years to come. How would that help *us* in *our* family? It wouldn't have helped us at all. What good would come from it? Nothing. It would have torn their families apart—like ours. We are torn, and they would be, too. Their babies would no longer have their daddy, and that wasn't our intention.

Our case needed to set a precedence for any other possible future incidents.

Surely, this won't happen ever again.

Thirty days or more of jail—that was all Jack requested, and I agreed. We wanted accountability. After all, thirty days in jail was not too much to ask when it came to the death of our little son.

Maybe we should have requested more days--or several years. Thirty days is nothing when it came to the death of our son.

Jack held the affidavit in his hands, a written statement about the crime scene and submitted by the OSBI, the Oklahoma State Bureau of Investigation, who helped the Noble Police Department and the Norman Police Department with investigations following the shooting.

For the past eight months, it seemed to us that the OSBI wrote the report to benefit the police officers, and Jack addressed the reasons we felt that way. As Jack read through the information, he pointed out the sections we felt were incorrect in the investigative report.

Jack read, "The report said the snake was venomous, but *we* learned on August 8, 2007, through an article in a newspaper, the snake was non-venomous."

So the police tried to say they had good reason to fire their gun in the city limits since there was a threat. But a non-venomous snake is not a threat.

Jack continued reading, "The snake was removed at 2:30 a.m. the following morning, on August 4 by a Norman Animal Control Officer. The birdhouse hung by one nail. So, he used a rake handle to push up on the bottom of the birdhouse and knocked the birdhouse to the ground. The control officer removed the snake with a tong-like instrument that he brought with him. The snake was still alive, and they froze it for evidence."

I shook my head in disbelief. *Why didn't the Noble police call the Norman Animal Control for help instead of shooting their pistol? It would have saved Austin's life.*

After our family cleared the brush, we could see the birdhouse from the dock, although there were few trees in the direct line from where the officer shot to the dock. They said we lived in a *forested* area, but that was not true. There was only brush, overgrown grass, and a few trees scattered here and there.

It looks like a park by our pond with beautiful fruit trees, so why would they say it is a forested area? Possibly, to make it look more like an "accident" rather than negligence.

"Another problem with the affidavit," Jack said, "is that it said all three police officers came to our front yard after Renee's initial screams, but only two officers came to our yard, and when they found out what happened, they neither implied nor admitted it was *them* who had shot the weapon. They offered us no help."

The police officer who shot the gun didn't come to our yard. I don't know where he was. The supervisor who I shook by the shoulders that day and the female police officer who reported to the snake first were the ones who jumped the fence and came to our house.

In our front yard, they appeared angry with me when they said, "Get over there and take care of your son!"

I could only think of one thing at a time, so I went to my son's side, but how would I have reacted if they told me they were the ones who shot my son? Even now, I shudder at the thought.

Jack continued, "Your Honor, I believe this OSBI report was written in bias toward the police officers to make them look innocent because it is public access and public knowledge. The people in our community need to know the truth, not the false statements from this report. Most of the report is true, but not all of it.

"The police officers said they attempted to use other weapons before the use of the firearm," Jack said, "but I brought photos we took of the crime scene. In these photos, you will see a rake, a hoe, and some hedge clippers down below the awning where the birdhouse was hanging. I believe the hoe would have worked in the successful removal of the snake. Wouldn't the long-handled hedge clippers have worked? I believe so, but no, they chose to shoot their gun instead."

Jack was determined to present the court with correct information, and he left the podium stand and took his seat beside me. I thought he did an excellent job with his testimony.

Next, it was my turn. *What should I say? I will never be able to forgive these police officers. They have torn my family apart, and life will never be the same.*

I approached the podium with shaking knees and my head pounding with anger. I wasn't even sure I could make it to the podium, but I did, and I held the sides for support.

Once I was in place in front of the courtroom, I intended to glance at the judge so I could address him with my comments. At the last minute, though, I turned my body and looked into the police officers' eyes as I spoke. I wanted them to see the burden I had carried the past eight months and would carry for the rest of my life.

Tears burned my eyes. My chin quivered, and I did my best to be strong and speak with boldness, but I began sobbing before I could utter a single word. I tried to be strong like when I spoke at Austin's funeral, but I was too hurt and angry at the officers. *How dare they take my son away from me?* I wanted them to know first-hand how their mistake had ruined my life forever.

Through tears and sniffles, I somehow found the courage to address the court. "I am Renee Cheri Haley, and I am the mama of Austin

Gabriel Haley. My baby boy was five years, nine months, and ten days old at the time his life was stolen away from me, and it was all because of the decisions *you* police officers made.

"People often ask how I am doing since the shooting," I said. I always struggle to answer that question because I feel angry, devastated, sad, distraught, and in a never-ending emotional turmoil with a constant battle raging in my mind. Is that something I want to tell people? Is that something they wanted to hear when they are nice enough to ask? Did they expect a simple, 'I'm fine,' when I was far from fine?

"Our family and friends felt the pain of our loss, and life goes on for everyone else, but not for us."

My gaze tore into each officer as I sat across the room from them. "My son was ripped from my arms by you, and I can no longer hold him, feel his hugs, or kiss his little cheeks."

"Most of the time, my mind won't allow me to dwell on the pleasant memories and the tremendous closeness we had. Austin and I had a special bond, and we did everything together. He was the first baby to make me a mom.

"Instead of peaceful thoughts going through my mind, I often see flashes of the horrific nightmare that took place on August 3, 2007, one day after my birthday."

I turned to address the judge for a moment. "Your Honor, if it had been me who killed a child out of negligence and recklessness as these police officers did, I can guarantee I would have been handcuffed and placed in jail.

"My child is dead, and they may walk away with no jail time and still be able to continue working as police officers after a few, short years of a possible suspension. We don't know what will happen with them, but that's what their attorneys have requested. If Austin were *your* child, Your Honor, would you be okay with that decision?

"These police officers faced many different decisions on that fateful summer day. They could have chosen to not shoot inside city limits since houses are lined up one after another in our neighborhood. There was no threat, *no* imminent danger, the homeowner wasn't even home when the police officers were there. So, there was *no* reason for them to shoot.

"If I had forgotten to put a seat belt on Austin and he died in a car accident, I would have been handcuffed and taken to jail that day."

I turned again to speak to the police officers, "Now, I have to watch as my little son, Dalton, grieves for his brother every day. And this precious baby I'm now pregnant with, who will be born in two months, won't even know their oldest brother, Austin. The baby won't know how wonderful his hugs were or know the joy of having Austin crawl in the crib to read a book. This baby won't hear his voice saying, "'I love you so much.'" Dalton got to experience all these things and misses them every single day."

My eyes bored into the police officers' eyes the entire time I spoke.

Most of the time, they sat behind their table showing no emotion, except occasionally when their faces might turn red, and they would look away for a few seconds.

I continued talking straight toward them. "Are you guilty? Do you want to apologize to me? Are you angry because I am blaming you? Look into my eyes and hear every word I say. I need you to know and feel my pain!"

I told them the story—the entire story from *my* point of view—of how I experienced the loss of Austin on August 3, 2007. I told them about how Austin continued crying that morning, saying, "Mama, it's going to be a very bad day. I am going to miss you, Daddy, and Dalton so much."

I wanted these police officers to know about Austin's nightmares. "You see, ever since he was three years old, he had recurring nightmares of a police officer, like you, taking him away from us and hurting him. I reassured him the best I knew how. I told Austin police officers were there to *help* and *protect*, that they would never *hurt* him."

*"The police would never hurt you, Son—*those words have been an ominous whisper in my ears so many times since the tragedy."

I told them about the list of three wishes Austin had—playing on the swings, digging in the sandbox, and going to the pond. We completed his list.

"I'm so thankful we finished his list before you shot your gun, but did you know before the shots were fired, I heard your giggles and laughter coming from the neighbor's backyard? Yes, I heard it while the kids and I built tunnels in the sandbox. I asked the boys to be quiet a minute because something may be wrong at our neighbor's house, and I heard all of you laughing as you said something about a snake, fire, and a hole.

I couldn't tell what you were saying, but according to today's testimony, I now realize, you were discussing the plan of yelling, 'fire in the hole' and shooting at the snake. You were laughing about it! It was all a joke to you. That laughter will never leave me as I recall the final precious moments before my son's death."

I took a drink of water and a few deep breaths and then continued, "I didn't know specific information about the incident because the police department refused to give me information or evidence when I requested it, but I was *finally* able to get a copy of the recorded radio control call, which gave specific times and events of that terrible night.

"At 7:42 p.m., the neighbor called the police station about the snake, and a female police officer reported to the scene at 7:46 p.m. She decided she needed assistance, and at 7:51 p.m., the log stated the police officer tried to reach the homeowner where the snake was located but failed.

"At 7:53 p.m., the female officer requested the assistance of two other officers to help, and you both arrived on the scene at 8:00 p.m. The log didn't state when the two shots were fired, but it must have been sometime between 8:05 p.m. and 8:10 p.m. because my 911 recording was logged at 8:12 p.m.

"So, officers of your department were sent to figure out the best plan for getting rid of a snake stuck in a birdhouse from 7:42 p.m. until around 8:10 p.m., which was twenty-eight minutes total. Think about that. You had twenty-eight minutes to make an informed decision on how to get a snake out of a birdhouse, but the best you two officers could come up with was shooting the snake while the third female officer stood back and watched. Did you once stop to think maybe you should call Animal Control before shooting? Did you stop to think there might be children playing in the field behind the birdhouse where you were standing? Or adults tinkering in workshops, fishing, or mowing? You were in the middle of a neighborhood—a location where people lived and worked and played. Did you ever stop to think your shooting the snake could be harmful to people? And then when your first bullet didn't kill the snake, you took a second shot and *still* didn't kill the snake!"

"What I want to know is why? Why didn't you think about the people you serve in this community and what was best for them? Aren't you trained to protect and not cause harm?

"The log also stated a medical air evacuation team was waiting for the ambulance to transport Austin from our house to Noble High School. The helicopter arrived at the school at 8:25 p.m. but the air evacuation team refused to transport him until 8:38 p.m. That was thirteen minutes that he needed to be at the hospital! Why did it take so long to get my son to the hospital? Our family doesn't understand.

"When Jack and I arrived at the hospital, Austin wasn't there because, unknown to us, they transported him by ambulance instead. The doctor had to be one who told us the decision was made because there wasn't hope of saving Austin. Not you. Why couldn't you have let us know that plans had changed, and he would be taken by ambulance instead? The wait was absolute misery for us. It was complete torture.

"Were you all discussing your plan of what to do or say while you were at the school rather than bringing him to the hospital right away? We asked to ride in the ambulance and the helicopter, but you wouldn't allow it. We needed to be with our dying son."

"Why did you do this to our family?" I asked, sobbing, "Why did you kill our baby boy?"

At the end of my testimony, I vacated the podium and returned to my seat even angrier at the officers who shot and killed my son.

I dwelled on each piece of evidence and the number of things I wanted to say to those police officers grew, but my time of fifteen minutes—the time the judge allotted to each speaker—was over.

Tragedy

Out of respect to the court, I allowed my dad to take his turn next. As we crossed paths, I noticed his face was pale, and he couldn't seem to place one foot in front of the other as he walked to the front. I reached over and squeezed his hand in hopes of giving him strength. He was a grieving grandpa.

Because he was an attorney for over twenty years, it felt familiar seeing him in court. He was a good attorney, and he hadn't lost a single jury trial in fifteen years.

However, this time he seemed different in the courtroom. Rather than speaking with a strong voice as I heard him for years, his voice was now tired and weak. He could barely speak the words.

"Austin was my—was just—was a happy baby. He came to see me and my wife, his grandma, several times a week. During our time together, we often went to the pond. He wanted me to take him there that day. I knew he would want to go when I drove up in the Polaris. It's something we did two or three times a week.

"That day, Papa Jim, his great-grandfather, stood behind him putting a worm on his hook when the shot rang out. I had no idea it was a blast from a police officer's gun until much later in the evening. I thought it was someone's attempt to murder me or my whole family."

He echoed all the things Jack and I had mentioned during our testimony about how ridiculous the police officers' decisions were that day, and he also requested at least thirty days in jail for the officers' consequence.

"I can't believe the report we read suggested the gunfire was the result of a ricochet. From the beginning of the report, our family felt it was a straight shot from the birdhouse to the dock, but it seemed like the evidence was always slanted for the benefit of the police officers,' Dad said from the stand.

"Because of this, we felt we were compelled to conduct our own investigation in search of the truth. We went to the pond area with a mower, and we removed the brush and grass from the neighbor's back fence to the location on the dock where my grandson stood. We set up a transit, a telescope mounted on a tripod used for surveying the position of lines and angles, and sure enough, it was a straight line. It wasn't a ricochet like the report showed at all, and we didn't have to remove any large trees."

Dad took a deep breath and continued. "I resented the police officers interrogating me at the hospital. I was within ten feet of my dead grandson's body, and police officers tried to accuse *me* of killing him. I hope nobody ever goes through that pain. I suppose it was all to protect the police officers. The Norman Police Department knew who had shot my grandson. They knew it. Why did they try to pin the blame on me?'

My dad broke into tears. I don't believe he could take the burden anymore and still felt tremendous pain from Austin's death.

He vacated the stand and rejoined my mom at his seat in the audience and sobbed. The judge moved on to the next testimony.

Next, Jack's sister came to the podium. To begin, she read a note Jack's mom had written:

Tragedy

"Isn't a policeman supposed to know the streets of his town? Those houses have been there for years, but they were so eager to kill a snake, they disregarded the danger to human life.

"Jack lost his firstborn son. He'll never have the chance to teach him all the things a man wants to teach his son. He'll miss out on all the milestones of Austin's life: his school days, his graduation, his marriage, and his children. It's gone forever.

"Austin's poor mom, bless her. They killed her son the day after her thirty-first birthday. She's a teacher, and she'll see other people's children growing up. She'll help them achieve their goals, but her child is gone forever, robbed of his life by people sworn to protect him.

"What we seek today isn't revenge on the police department but justice for Austin. Someone must do something to stop a calamity like this from happening again.

"I am appalled we don't have better standards for our police officers. My son, Kenneth, was a police officer for several years, and his standards were high. He enforced the law, but he also lived by the law. A law that applies to an ordinary citizen should apply to an officer.

"If it's wrong for a civilian to shoot a gun in a residential area, it is wrong for a police officer to shoot one without looking, without seeing, without caring for what might be in the trajectory of the bullet.

"Shouldn't they have attempted a less deadly approach before resorting to gunfire? The rake, hoe, and hedge clippers were at their feet. They should have used them. It would have saved Austin's life."

During my mom's intense testimony, she held up the birdhouse for everyone to see. It was wooden and painted red. "The non-venomous snake was stuck in this little hole in the front of the birdhouse. The snakes' head was hanging down about a foot and ten inches, and the head was moving.

"Three police officers were on the scene that day, but only two police officers are charged because the first female officer didn't say or do anything as they shot their gun. It wasn't her plan, but she watched as they senselessly, carelessly, and negligently attempted to shoot the snake.

"The night Austin died was an absolute nightmare, and the horrendous loss our family has suffered is never-ending. I'm sure the entire family would agree that a part of all of us died that night when Austin passed. Since his tragic death, we feel such a void in our family, and we always will.

"Why did you break the law?" Mom asked. "The law states it's illegal to shoot a firearm within city limits unless there is imminent danger. There was *no* imminent danger in our situation, which means my grandson died in vain."

I let out a loud sigh because my mom's words were so true. *My baby died in vain.*

Everyone in the courtroom sat in silence. There was no movement except for my mom shuffling through her pages of typed notes and sniffles from our family crying.

Mom continued, "You relied on a neighbor to look on the internet for you to determine if the snake was venomous or not. Using the neighbor to look up the snake was a very poor source. How did you know you could trust this neighbor's judgment as to if this snake was venomous or not? You listened to our twelve-year-old neighbor and her mother who said the snake was venomous. She was twelve—*a young child*—who looked up the information on the internet. How dare you take the advice of a child?

"Why did you break your training? You were trained to not only know your target but also know what's behind the target. Not one of you three police officers bothered to walk a few more yards to the other side of the fence to see if anybody was there before you shot. So, you broke the law, and you broke your training.

"As police officers, maps of Noble were at your disposal. You should have known there is a huge pond down there. The supervisor has worked at the department for five years, so he had to know there was a pond there. And where there's a pond, there are always people.

"Not one of you officers spoke up and said, 'Maybe we better not shoot here because this house is within city limits. We might kill somebody. Maybe we better think about this before we get this .357 automatic pistol out and shoot.'

"If you at least used a shotgun, my grandson might still be alive today because the shotgun's bullet wouldn't have traveled near as far as your pistol. According to our family's research, a shotgun has an effective range of about thirty-eight yards with buckshot, and your pistol could've continued more than a mile!

"Your decision was poor judgment, and it was negligent and senseless. It's beyond what we can imagine.

Mom kept right on talking and between all my sobs, I was so proud of her. "If you police officers had fired your weapon out of self-defense to prevent getting shot or to stop a criminal and accidentally killed Austin, we would have been devastated, but at least it would have made more sense. This was all because of a non-venomous snake—stuck in a birdhouse because it had eaten an egg—an egg! If you would have stopped to use common sense and logic that day, my grandson would still be with us.

"You should have used your ears, too. Didn't you hear Jack's music blasting from his workshop? He was closer than anyone to you. Could you not hear my husband yell that someone was down at the pond? No you didn't because you didn't bother to stop and listen to what was happening around you.

"An Animal Control Officer from Norman, our neighboring town removed the snake at 2:30 a.m. the following morning. If you thought the rat snake was so dangerous to the community—if it was so dangerous as to warrant risking a fatal shooting—why did you leave the rat snake to go to my daughter and son-in-law's home after you heard all the screaming? If it was so dangerous, why did you leave the snake there that long?"

The officers' faces turned red, and they looked down at the floor.

"Whether you're a police officer or not, any person who breaks the law should be held accountable," Mom said. "Police officers sometimes are negligent with guns because they don't worry about the law coming after them. After all, the law typically doesn't punish their own, and that's not fair. Just because they wear a uniform and have a gun on their hip does not make them any better than everyone else.

"Don't get me wrong. There are a lot of good police officers out there, and our family recognizes that. Many of them have come forward and offered their sincerest condolences, but the police who broke law and policies put in place to protect not only themselves but also the innocent people they serve, deserve some jail time for sure."

I agree. There are many good police officers who make wise decisions. We need police officers, but if they break the law, they should have the same consequence as anyone else.

"While we are here on earth, there will always be a void in our family. The only hope we have regarding my grandson, Austin Haley, is we will see him again in Heaven, where Jesus is taking care of him right now.

"Oh, how I miss you, my precious little five-year-old grandson, Austin Haley."

My mom did a great job with her testimony. She mentioned everything that lay heavy on my mind, and she spoke the words for me that I didn't have time to say.

Several other family members expressed their feelings about Austin's death: Papa Jim, MaMaw, my sister, my sister's husband, my aunt, my husband's other sister, my husband's brother, and a good friend from the community.

After months of waiting for some form of punishment, the moment had arrived. The judge was ready to make his decision. There was no jury—the judge was going to make the final decision.

"I have heard the state's offer of proof, and the statements made by the family of Jack and Renee Haley, and based on those things, I find both defendants *guilty* as charged."

The courtroom remained quiet except for a few gasps from both sides of the audience.

In agreement with the judge's decision, Jack and I shook our heads. We knew in our hearts they were guilty from day one, but I'm not sure it helped our feelings any. Maybe it should have. I figured there would be joy in my heart as I heard the word, *guilty*, but instead, there wasn't any joy. Just loneliness, sadness, and anger.

I glanced at the two officers' families, and I knew they were distraught by the look on their faces. They were crying, and somehow, I felt concerned for them. None of these decisions were made by the police officers' families. I'm sure they were worried the officers would be going to jail for a while. Maybe a long while.

Judge Lucas continued, "This is the most emotional testimony I've heard in the past forty-four years of doing law.

"For that reason, having found the defendants guilty as charged I'm going to recess this hearing until Monday, March 31st, for judgment and sentence.'"

What? Recess? We have to wait another weekend before we know his decision? I couldn't believe my ears.

"May there be comfort in knowing that someone so special will never be forgotten."

—Julie Hebert—

The Final Decision

On Monday, my entire family once again returned to the courtroom on pins and needles. As we walked up the sidewalk into the courthouse, I heard birds chirping. Something about their chirps irritated me instead because those were happy sounds, and happiness was yanked from my life all those months ago.

My heart raced as I entered the courtroom with Jack and my family surrounding me. I longed for the simplicity of a few windows where I could feel the sunlight, but the room felt dark and dreary. My heart was too sad for rays of light anyway.

After taking our seats, I noticed people whispering around the room. The palms of my hands were sweating, and I felt nervous once again. I looked at people's faces. Both families appeared sad and nervous. I couldn't help but notice the gray paneled walls, and the huge seal of the State of Oklahoma that was behind the judge's empty black leather chair.

What will the judge decide? What will he tell us after he takes his seat and bangs his gavel?

Police officers work hand-in-hand with the judicial system, and it was obvious our situation was no different.

Most of the time, Jack and I felt alone. We didn't have an attorney. The state of Oklahoma's District Attorney and the Assistant District Attorney was not ours like we thought, but they were appointed to the state. They should have been an advocate to us, though, and it didn't feel that way.

I leaned forward and whispered to my dad in the seats in front of us. "Dad, why is the District Attorney on the police officer's side rather than ours? At least, it feels that way to me. They are always standing and talking to the police officers over at their table rather than coming to us."

"I know, Honey. I suppose the reason is that police officers help the District Attorney keep their job. It's all because of the FOP. The District Attorney will never go against that organization, no matter what the case is about."

"What? What is that—FOP?"

"It's the Fraternal Order of Police. If the District Attorney goes against the FOP, they could lose the vote of being District Attorney. They need the support of the community and the police in the county. It's all about politics."

"But, it's so unfair. They are helping the police officers, and they're making deals with their attorneys, so the District Attorney's job can be saved? That's so wrong."

I shook my head in disbelief.

For the past few months of meeting with the District Attorney, Jack and I asked if we could hire our own attorney, but the laws didn't allow it since it was a criminal case against police officers, and it involved the state. Our hands were tied.

My dad explained things the best he could as our intermediary attorney, but it was difficult through his own grief, and most legal meetings were hidden from our family. Each legal step added to the dark storm looming over our family because it was all challenging to understand what was happening. We had no council sitting next to us in the courtroom, and no one was there to answer legal questions, except for my dad.

My dad would have understood what was happening and could've explained the legal steps to us if the District Attorney's office included him and my family in the meetings. From the beginning, however, the Defense Attorneys and the District Attorney's office made deals behind closed doors. They didn't want our family to be included.

We didn't feel we were receiving help from anybody dealing with our case: the police, the investigative team dealing with the crime scene, or our own advocates.

I sighed, thinking, *where is our help? It seems everyone wants to help the police officers, but it was our son who was shot and killed. Please, God, help us.*

There was a definite tension between the District Attorney's office and our family. We didn't agree with the plea bargain they must have made with the Police Officers' attorneys behind closed doors. We didn't even know about the meetings when they were discussing our case. They could have called us or written a letter, but they didn't until the meeting was over.

The *plea bargain*, an arrangement made between the prosecutor and the defendant weeks or months earlier, would only give both officers a two-year deferred sentence, as well as a five hundred dollar fine that would be given to a victim's compensation fund—not us.

We didn't believe the plea bargain was firm enough. The "sweet heart deal," as my dad called it, allowed the police officers to plead guilty and receive a more lenient sentence. The agreement made between the attorneys from the opposing sides was for the officers to receive a *deferred sentence*. In other words, our case would be dismissed after the police officers completed their probation period of two years.

We didn't know what questions to ask my dad, but we were trying to understand the next step. Could there be jail time added for these police officers? If so, how long? What are the other possibilities of sentencing from here? Could there be prison time? Can the judge decide something different than what the attorneys decided? My dad didn't have time to answer our many questions.

The courtroom silenced. The attorneys took their seats as the judge walked in and sat down. He took several seconds to put his glasses on and glance over his paperwork. The oppressive silence settled in and ruled the room.

I held my breath as the judge welcomed people to the proceeding and gave last-minute instructions, most of which I'm not even sure I heard. In my mind, I screamed at him to hurry and tell me his decision.

I released my breath through pursed lips as the judge's eyes looked at our family and then the officers' families.

"The officers' actions were grossly negligent," he said. "They exercised poor judgment and outrageous decision-making skills. The Haley family is justified in their outrage."

My heart was beating like a kettle drum. I concentrated on every word he said.

"The officers' decision to shoot the firearm under the circumstances was a tragically wrong decision. Inappropriate, negligent, outrageous, and inexcusable are not strong enough words to describe what happened on the fateful day of August 3, 2007.

"The act of shooting the snake, though not made with intent to kill another human being, was a deliberate act of poor judgment."

The judge turned his head to focus on the officers that sat before him. Every head in the place turned in unison in anticipation of the judge's next words. "Gentlemen, I know you are not cold-blooded murderers, but the decisions you made were negligent. I reject the plea bargain that the state has given. I feel it should be a harsher sentence."

Jack and I looked at each other and our eyes widened. We didn't say any words, but I knew we were thinking *a harsher sentence? Like thirty days in jail?*

We locked eyes with the judge as he said the next few words. Therefore, for the next *two-and-a-half years,* the court decrees that the rookie, the one who was given the order to shoot from the supervising officer, will no longer serve his community as a police officer. Likewise, for the next *five* years, the supervisor will no longer serve his community as a police officer.

"Both officers are ordered to one day per week of community service, eight hours a day for twenty-six weeks, so that's half a year. The community service must be completed at either the local animal control facility or a zoo.

"The judgment I am making today will be deferred. This case will be expunged after five years. The court is adjourned."

I didn't understand. *Deferred? Expunged after five years? What does all this mean?*

I glanced at the officers after the sentence was passed, but I couldn't see their reaction since they were sitting in front of us on the opposite side of the courtroom. I could see the back of their necks getting red. As I looked at the police officers' wives and families, they seemed relieved.

After the judge left, I felt confused. We needed to ask questions to our attorney, but they weren't sitting with us. Instead, they were standing once again with the police officers and the opposing counsel. It seemed they had all of the attorneys, including ours.

I looked at Jack in disbelief, wondering what all this meant.

Our family exited the courtroom together and walked into the hallway.

I asked my dad, "What does deferred mean?"

My dad looked at the floor in emotional exhaustion. "Honey, *deferred* means if the police officers complete their probation without incident, Austin's case will be dismissed."

"Dismissed? Why? That's ridiculous. I heard them say the word expunged, too. What does that mean?"

"*Expunged* means no record will be kept of your case."

"No record? No record at all? But, Austin's case must be used in the future to stop something like this from happening again. Why would they throw out our case as if Austin's life doesn't matter?"

Tragedy

My heart sank, and I leaned my head onto Jack's shoulder in exhaustion. My fists clenched and a waterfall of emotions fell from my eyes. Angriness, bitterness, rage, and sadness escaped my eyes one drop at a time. But, with my feelings, there was no escape. I didn't want to anyway. I was at a loss for words, and anger spoke for me.

So—no jail time was given—only community service. *My heart ached.* I was so angry with the police officers I couldn't see straight, but I didn't say much. I kept my feelings of anger trapped inside—like a shaken bottle of pop about to explode.

There was no lawsuit due to the existing laws that protected the police officers, nor were there statewide or nationwide changes as a result of Austin's death.

The only thing that could be considered a positive change in the system is that some police departments across the United States now use Austin's story as a reminder to police officers of what *not* to do in situations similar to ours.

But, how will the police departments even know about our situation once our case is expunged from the record?

Our case concerning our son, Austin Gabriel Haley, will be expunged, and his name erased from every law record in existence.

And once that happens, these police officers who shot our son will be free to become officers again. How is that even possible?

"The reality is that you will grieve forever. You will not 'get over' the loss of a loved one; you'll learn to live with it. You will heal and you will rebuild yourself around the loss you have suffered. You will be whole again, but you will never be the same. Nor should you be the same nor would you want to."

—Elisabeth Kubler-Ross—

How Do I Forgive?

As soon as the court sentencing was completed and the court adjourned, reeling from the unexpected decision of no jail time for the officers—only community service—Jack and I fled the courthouse through the back exit. Neither of us wanted to deal with the media who were crowded around the front entrance with their microphones and cameras, ready to ask questions.

Our footsteps echoed back at us as we rushed through the dim hallway. Jack and I didn't speak. We didn't want anyone to infringe on our thoughts of the day. We spoke enough in the hearing and were exhausted from reliving Austin's death through the testimonies in court.

As we walked, I could barely put one foot in front of the other, and I could tell by Jack's body language that he felt the same way.

I felt an urgency to speak with Jack, to ask him his opinions about the decisions made by the court, but the discussion would have to wait until we were alone.

Reliving each detail of Austin's death brought me back to that terrifying moment when my dad said those life-altering words, "Honey—someone shot Austin—right in the head—I don't think he's going to make it." Even now as I thought the words, I wanted to scream.

Life is not fair! How dare police officers take my son away from me! They didn't even get one day of jail time. If it were me who killed somebody, I would be in jail right now and would be there for the rest of my life!

The rage I felt toward the officers was insurmountable. Now the court hearing was over, and I should've felt immeasurable relief, but no sentencing or lack thereof would return my little boy back to my arms.

Jack and I took two or three turns through the hallways, trying to find the back door. I heard a few muffled voices as we neared the exit.

"I hope that's not the media," I whispered to Jack.

"Me too. I wouldn't know what to say to them right now. I'm too angry."

As we rounded the corner, we expected to see cameras and microphones. Instead, we faced a family of five people. A sense of relief flooded me, and I intended to rush past them without acknowledgment, but as one of them in the group turned toward us, I paused because he looked familiar. *That's when I recognized him.*

My heart pounded because I was now face-to-face with the rookie police officer who pulled the trigger, resulting in my son's death! My hroat closed, and I trembled in disbelief. My face burned, and I gasped 'or air. I stood frozen like a statue.

Every nerve in my body jumped and a myriad of emotions overtook ne—anger, fear, sadness, depression, and exhaustion spewed out like a aunched cannonball. I reached out to hit him while my mind devised he many ways to tell him off. I wanted to slam him against the wall.

Wait—I can't hit him. If I do, I'll get thrown in jail or prison while ne walks free.

didn't expect the course of events that happened next.

And just like that, the officer collapsed to his knees in front of us, egging for forgiveness. Streams of tears flowed down his cheeks.

"I am *so* sorry. I wish I had done something different that day. I am o sorry. No words could *ever* express how sorry I am." His eyes were umble and hurt. He was distraught, and I could tell he had lost veight. As angry as I was, I couldn't deny that he was sincerely pologetic.

Jack and I stood silent, unsure of what to say, and the officer looked t us with wide eyes. Again, he begged for forgiveness. "I'm so sorry. 'm so sorry. I didn't mean to kill your little boy."

My grief-filled mind sank into complete despair, and I worked hard o stay on my feet. The burden of whether I would forgive this man was nore than my mind could bear.

I can't forgive you for pulling that trigger and killing my son. That vas a stupid choice! You shot my son because of a non-venomous snake stuck in a birdhouse! The whole situation was nonsense and never should've happened.

Those were the words I wanted to say, but as soon as they crossed my mind, something unexpected happened. A detailed picture or a vision, I'm not sure which, overcame my mind.

Jesus hung on a cross with nails through his hands and feet. He had a crown of thorns on his head. They spat on Him as blood gushed from his body, and he was cursed, laughed at, and persecuted. It must have been difficult for him to take all the pain, but he still managed to say, "Father forgive them, for they know not what they do."

Even through all the pain Jesus endured, He forgave those people How?

My heart softened as I remembered the words Jesus said. "Father forgive them, for they know not what they do."

How did Jesus do that?

Jack and I stood there and broke into tears. We were silent because any words we spoke would be inadequate. Standing before us was the man who had pulled the trigger and killed our son.

Despite my hurt and pain, somewhere deep in my heart, I saw this officer's pain.

I looked at Jack for a split second and nodded. We reached down and lifted this man to his feet, hugged him, and I spoke the words couldn't imagine saying, "We forgive you. We'll be praying for you."

How did we do that? We gave the man who killed our son a hug What were we thinking?

It wasn't easy, but we cried with the officer and shared each other' pain.

Right then and there, the hatred and bitterness I had toward this man somehow vanished.

I'll never be okay with the decision he made that day, but I had forgiven him, and more than anything, I wanted him to feel comfort.

Whenever I reached toward the police officer, I felt as if I was telling him, *I know you did not shoot my son with wrong-doing in your heart. I know it was not in your heart to take him away from his daddy, little brother, and me. I forgive you.*

As I walked out of the courtroom that day, I decided I would no longer carry the burden of the anger.

Settling in the car to drive home, I still couldn't believe I forgave the police officers who killed my son. I was so angry with him and the other officers for the past eight months that it felt like another being living inside of me—an angry, hurt, bitter being I didn't like living inside of me.

I'm not even sure it was a "conscious" choice I made, but with the image of Jesus flooding my mind like a river washing my soul, it was an automatic feeling in my heart. I knew forgiveness was the right thing to do, and I felt God was pleased with that decision. Jack felt the same way.

"Grief never ends . . . But it changes. It's a passage, not a place to stay. Grief is not a sign of weakness, nor a lack of faith . . . It is the price of love."

—Elizabeth I—

The Journey Called "Life"

 I don't know how I found it within my weak self to forgive the police officers. Before I decided to forgive that day, I had sunk into a deep, dark prison—otherwise known as depression. I was sad and grieving, lonesome and troubled. The worst feeling of all, though, was the anger I carried inside my heart. It was a massive weight on my shoulders I had to carry around along with all the other feelings I experienced after the death of my first-born son.

After the encounter with the police officers at the back door of the courthouse, I felt lighter. I could breathe again without gasping for air. I knew I had done the right thing. I don't know how I did it, but I did the right thing.

Forgiveness wasn't only a one-time occurrence. It was recurring; there was another time I will never forget. It was late April 2008, and I was having a weak moment. I was pleading to God to take the pain away from my heart. I had already forgiven the police officers, so I felt all anger should dissipate, never return. But, forgiveness wasn't wrapped in a pretty package for me. It wasn't easy. A heaviness settled in my chest that I couldn't explain. Life before, Life now. Is it even possible to move on from something like this?

It's not supposed to be this way.

I took a walk through the trails on our land to help subside the bitterness and resentment toward the officers, and the sun blazed across the sky. It hadn't rained much, so that afternoon when I crossed the field, I felt stalks of grass crackle and break beneath my feet. My heart was breaking, too, so it felt right.

My choice of moving forward was a battlefield. Moving on was a journey. I'd wrestled with forgiveness day by day, and on this day, I felt defeated. A scream rushed through my veins, and no matter how desperate I was to keep it in, I couldn't.

I found a rock on the ground, so I picked it up and threw it as far as I could. I hoped it made a loud sound as it fell to the ground, like the screaming in my thoughts, but it didn't. I couldn't hear it much at all. So, I threw a bigger one.

I walked another few minutes, but my legs felt too weak to stand. I leaned over, picked up a stick, and began to draw in the red Oklahoma dirt. I drew designs and circles as I became deep in thought.

Healing will take time, but I must move forward. Can I get there? Forgiveness is necessary. I've already forgiven the officers at the courthouse when he dropped to his knees and pleaded for forgiveness. So, why do I have to forgive them on a daily basis? It should be easier than this, God, but it's soooo hard.

I etched the words, "How do I truly forgive?" with the stick I had in my hands.

I didn't expect an answer, but God found a way to give it to me anyway.

When I stood up and was about to walk again, I noticed the path made a fork with two trails. *Which path am I going to take? Which way should I go? The decision was divided. My mind felt like it was going to explode.*

The one on the left would be difficult to take because it was covered with interlocking vines of thorns. There was a path, but it seemed rejected by life long ago. It didn't even appear that deer or other animals could take the walk through the rough terrain, not easily anyway. The thorns reminded me of hate, bitterness, resentment, and unforgiveness.

These were some of the things I was still feeling, though. *Should I walk that path? I have every right to feel that way.*

Across the fork to the right, I noticed the other path. It looked peaceful, and there was a creek running through it. I could hear the gentle water flowing, so I walked up to it and watched the water move for a long time. Eventually, I took my shoes and socks off and felt the cool water between my toes. My decision was made at that moment. I wanted to take the easier path of life. I could tell it wasn't going to be perfect, but somehow, there was more light peeking through the branches of the trees as I glanced upward, and it seemed a little less difficult to tread.

Somehow, the flowing water I dipped my feet into brought healing to my heart and mind.

As I walked a little further on the path, I saw a huge tree. I studied the tree next to the creek. It was tall, and the leaves were becoming full in the spring. Then, I looked down at the bottom of the tree. The roots appeared to be deep. I looked to the sky, and I cried loudly. "God, help me be like this tree. I want to forgive the officers with my whole heart. I want my roots to grow deep in You and for Your love to surround me. May my life become Yours. I want to take Your path in life. It may not always be easy, but You can help me through. I only see what the human mind can imagine. But, God, You are building something I cannot even fathom. Allow forgiveness to flow through me."

I leaned hard on the tree, and I wept. Something deep was happening within me.

It was a life-altering experience.

I felt lighter, and after slipping back on my socks and shoes, I started walking back to the house. But, in my heart and mind, I stayed on the path that God planned for me. Forgiveness was like the fork in the land. Should I forgive or not? Holding onto unforgiveness and bitterness wasn't diminishing my pain. It was multiplying, and it was the enemy of my soul.

It was at that moment, I stopped asking God, "why" and I began asking God, "What now?" Then, the Lord's Prayer entered my mind:

"Our Father which art in Heaven, hallowed be thy name. Thy kingdom come, thy will be done on Earth, as it is in Heaven. Give us this day our daily bread. And forgive us our debts, as we forgive our debtors. And lead us not into temptation, but deliver us from evil: For hine is the kingdom, and the power, and the glory, forever. Amen." Matthew 6: 9-13)

t wasn't long before others crossed my path who were hurting and ingry. I recall when one of my friends lost her child. She was desperate 'or help and answers. She was bitter, and she had every right to feel hat way. Her young son passed away due to child abuse at the hands of ier son's babysitter. I recall her asking me a difficult question, "Do I iave to make the choice to forgive, or is it a feeling I will eventually iave?"

I believe forgiveness is a choice we make. Our motivation for 'orgiving someone increases with our obedience to God and His :ommand to forgive. God instructs us to forgive as the Lord forgave us. 'Bear with each other and forgive whatever grievances you may have igainst one another. Forgive as the Lord forgave you" (Colossians 3:13).

Another friend of mine had dealt with abuse all during her child-iood. She has held resentment and heartache for many years; now, he's an adult. There is no family support, and it's difficult for her to :nvision what forgiveness would feel like. "How do I forgive when I lon't feel like it?"

We simply keep faith in God. No matter how difficult, we still must ie obedient to His Word. Many times, forgiveness goes against our iature, but we must still forgive by faith, whether we feel like it or not. 3y putting our trust in God, He will do a mighty work in us that needs to be done in order for true forgiveness to be complete. I believe God honors our desire to please Him and our commitment to obey Him.

It begins with small steps—reading the Bible, praying, and growing closer to Him each and every day. Our hearts, full of anger, strife, and bitterness begin to somehow change to a heart more like the Lord if we simply grow closer to Him. He completes the work in His time. Forgiving by faith is our job until the work of forgiveness, the Lord's job, is done in our hearts.

Another person once asked me, "How will we know if we have truly forgiven?"

We will know the work of forgiveness is complete when we experience the freedom that comes as a result. God lifts us out of bondage and sets us free of the burden of holding a grudge. Once a person truly forgives, the Lord sets him or her free of bitterness, resentment, and hurt that previously had a stronghold on our lives. Many times, forgiveness is a very slow process. It will come, but only if we allow it.

Forgiveness is sometimes a daily occurrence and a conscious choice. Forgiveness may require a lifetime of forgiving, but it is important. We must continue forgiving until everything becomes settled in our hearts.

"Why do we have to forgive?" was another question that I had encountered.

The best reason to forgive is that Jesus commanded us to forgive. We learn from Scripture that if we don't forgive, neither will we be forgiven: "For if you forgive men when they sin against you, your heavenly Father will also forgive you. But if you do not forgive men their sins, your Father will not forgive your sins" (Matthew 6:14-16). The Lord notices when we put out the effort to forgive. In return, I believe many blessings will follow. He cares for us and loves us. He desires for is to be close to Him. "And when you stand praying, if you hold anything against anyone, forgive him, so that your Father in Heaven may forgive your sins" (Mark 11:25).

Finally, we forgive out of obedience to the Lord. It is a choice, a decision we make. As we forgive, we will begin to realize it is for our own good, and we receive the reward of forgiveness, which is freedom.

I continued the path of what life became. God never promised He would take all my pain away, but He let me know He walked with me when times were too difficult to bear.

God opened His griefcase in my heart, and I leaned hard on Him.

The road was still long and challenging, but as I carried the heavy load, I remembered to trust in God. I meditated on Him and the many good things He had brought our way. It helped me and my burdened heart, and it gave me light in my dark world.

It is hard to understand grief. At times, I mourned and cried a bucket of tears, but through the sadness and heartache, God helped restore my thoughts, and He gave me a sense of hope and joy once again. For, we had a baby coming in May!

"Forgiveness doesn't excuse their actions. Forgiveness stops their actions from destroying your heart."

—Karen Salmansohn—

Let Hope Begin

Several people reached out to our family after Austin passed. Some cried with me, and others gave me strength by being there. I will never forget the love and concern shown by so many of my family and friends. Many members of my family came from all over the United States, and they each showed us love in their own way. Sometimes it was a memory of Austin, and other times it may have been a hug or an encouraging word. No matter the type of love they showed, it gave me the strength to continue.

From the internet also came many forms of encouragement. For example, Kathy Spivey took photographs of Austin she found on the internet from various news articles and added angel wings to his image.

Another digitally-altered photo showed Austin looking up at Jesus with a large staircase entering Heaven. It was beautiful.

She also created pictures of the pond that looked so peaceful with an angel statue out front and Austin sitting on the dock. As she continued posting these beautiful pictures on the Internet, they helped bring me a sense of peace.

In the days following Austin's death, our family gathered at my parents' house, and friends and church family poured in, bringing in so much food, that we had to get a second refrigerator and set it on the front porch. I wanted everyone to have a snack and share the food with us, and I needed their concern and love.

Some sent flowers or plants.

We received hundreds of cards through the mail—many from people we did not know. Some heard our story on the news and sent cards from the east coast and the west coast. I did my best to keep a record of every single card, gift, item of food, and every flower.

In addition, I wanted to send everyone a thank-you card, as I did not want a single kindness to go without acknowledgement and thanks. Every single item brought me love and comfort. I was glad to remember each act of kindness.

Even though it took over a month to write a thank-you card to every person who showed us love, the time I spent doing it was important because we appreciated their kindness and generosity.

Even now, I still marvel at how much love and support our family received. It was wonderful, and it helped us more than words could ever express. To each of you who shared in our grief, we will never forget your kindness.

The community showed they cared in a variety of ways, and a few days later, a kind woman from our hometown in Noble heard about us losing our five-year-old son.

Laura King helped me during those worst moments of grief and despair, for she and her husband, Gary, had too experienced a tragedy with their six-year-old son, Justyn. He died in a boating accident in the year 2001. Laura called me on the phone several times after I had lost my precious little boy.

She listened as I told her about the fog of grief and depression hovering over me. She would uplift me with encouraging words such as these, "I don't know how, but somehow and someway, God will help you through this horrible time in your life. He will see you through." She sent me letters in the mail that had verses from the Bible—a bit of light for my broken heart. Her gracious and comforting words would echo through my ears during the moments I felt I could not go on another day.

Many times, I would read the same letter. I would pass them over for my husband to read. About that time, another comforting letter from her would be in the mailbox. I saved every letter she gave me.

When those times come, even today, when I need encouragement and strength, I will read her letters. I believe God sent her to uplift us. Her gracious kindness and love never ceased. Her words strengthened me and helped me. I was not alone—I had a friend who understood the pain, the turmoil, and the depression. I consider her a dear friend. Jack and I often discuss how blessed we feel by the gifts given to us.

All the gifts were amazing, and we will cherish them forever.

The city of Noble named a children's water park in Austin's memory. We had several meetings and decided on "Austin Haley's

Kool Kidz Splash" with assistance from Jack's mom, who thought of the name. It is such an honor.

Throughout the summer months, I like to sit on the bench at the splash pad and watch the kids play, including my own. When I glance up at the large, granite plaque on the back wall of the splash pad that has Austin's photo digitalized on it, my heart smiles. Ada Custom Memorials designed it as a donation. What a blessing, and we appreciate it so much.

On several occasions, while the splash pad was being built, Austin liked to drive by it to see if it was in operation yet.

Each time we passed by, he recognized if the construction crew had completed anything new. He was so excited and could not wait to play in the spraying water. Not long before they finished the splash pad Austin passed away.

As I sit out and watch all the little children play, sometimes I think I hear Austin's little laugh as if he is out there, too. We appreciate the city of Noble for considering Austin and us when naming the splash pad.

From the First State Bank in Noble, Kim King asked if she could donate money for the creation of the statue. With tears in our eyes, we told her, "We are so thankful for you thinking about us. Yes, we would love a statue of Austin."

She called John Gooden, a sculptor from Kingfisher, Oklahoma, and he was excited about the project and did a tremendous job. Much to Jack's and my satisfaction, the sculpture resembles Austin. It is amazing to look at it and realize, "Wow! That is a sculpture of our son."

The life-sized statue of Austin sits on a large granite boulder donated by Martin Marietta Materials and was placed on our property is a peaceful memorial. We sit with the statue at times and place our arms around it as if we are hugging Austin. What a gift this has been for our family.

About the time we thought all the gifts were subsiding, Chris Rogerson, a student from the Curtis Institute of Music in Philadelphia, sent us a letter. In the letter, he stated, "I saw Austin's tragic story on the news, and it moved me so much, I decided to write an orchestral piece called 'Noble Pond.'"

He invited us to go to Philadelphia and listen to the orchestra perform it. In the spring of 2008, as we sat in the audience watching the talented orchestra, tears filled our eyes.

Chris composed an outstanding piece that began with wind chimes representing a peaceful summer afternoon. The music built into a dramatic crescendo to express the tragedy itself. He expressed through music the emotions our family felt on August 3, 2007. "Noble Pond" was a wonderful gift. [Link: https://www.chrisrogerson.com/works/noble-pond].

Each person used their God-given talents and abilities, none of them less important than the other, to help through the healing process. A letter, kind word, written song or poem, a gentle hug, the creation of exceptional pictures and memorials all gave us strength.

The talents and abilities of beautiful gifts uplifted and encouraged us during difficult grief, as so many did during our terrible situation. All the acts of kindness were a blessing to us and helped our broken hearts.

"I learned that, with grief, you have to take it one day at a time and learn how to find the happiness amid the heartbreak."

—Adrienne C. Moore—

Happiness Returns

Nine months after Austin passed, we welcomed our third son, Gabriel Jeremiah Haley, on Friday, May 16, 2008. He was six pounds twelve ounces and nineteen inches long. *Gabriel* was Austin's middle name, and *Jeremiah* was from Austin's favorite verse:

"But blessed is the man who trusts in the Lord, whose confidence is in Him" (Jeremiah 17:7).

At the hospital, I told my dad, "Get ready. Your healing is coming."

He glanced up with a smile, but unmistakable sadness veiled his eyes. To this day, I remember that the look of sadness in my father's eyes startled me because I'd always seen those eyes brimming with happiness. "I hope you're right, Honey, but I don't know how that could be since there is no cure for Hepatitis C. I wish I could be healed of this terrible virus."

"I don't know how, Dad, but get ready. Austin prayed for you, too."

We praise God for Gabriel every day. When he was born, we wondered if Austin went to Heaven the night of August 3, 2007, to ask God for Gabriel. Maybe not, but we like to think so.

He had blond hair and blue eyes with a sweet personality. He was kind and gentle—a lot like the way Austin was. It helped Dalton when Gabriel was born. Dalton's eyes would brighten when he saw Gabriel, for he had a playmate once again. Dalton always felt like Gabriel was a gift from God himself, so he didn't have to be alone anymore.

After Austin passed, Dalton didn't speak for several minutes at a time throughout the day. I could tell he felt such loss and sorrow. As a mother, it grieved me to see my son under the burden of such sorrow knowing there was nothing I could do to make it better.

When Gabriel came along, we again saw snippets of happiness bubbling to the surface in Dalton. It brought much-needed joy to Jack and me to see his smiles and hear his laughter. He often expressed desires to give Gabriel a toy like Austin did with him.

He may not have realized it at the time, but he was stepping into Austin's role—

The role of big brother.

We watched in awe as Dalton took the lead in being the big

brother, and many times, he played with Gabriel the same way Austin had with him. Dalton would hand Gabriel a little toy sword, and clicking would commence as he and Dalton battled with all their might. Many times, I had to turn away as tears filled my eyes—this time, tears of gratitude—because laughter that disappeared from our home had returned.

When they dropped their swords with a clatter, Gabriel would chase until Dalton, finally, gave his little brother a big hug, "Oh, you got me, little brother!"

Then, they would sit in the recliner together while Dalton pretended to read Gabriel one of his favorite books.

Another of their favorite moments together was jumping on the trampoline outside our house. Gabriel didn't jump much because as Dalton jumped, Gabriel flew on his back and hopped up and down while Dalton did the jumping. Gabriel bellowed with his hearty laugh, which made Dalton laugh, too.

Watching them play, have fun, and laugh together was a healing balm to this grieving mother's soul.

When Gabriel hugged me, sweet and gentle, it felt "heaven-sent" from Austin himself.

One day, when Dalton was five years old and his little brother was two, Dalton spread Austin's bear blanket on the floor and asked Gabriel to sit on it next to him, so he could read books like *Elmo*. He would put his fingers through the puppet-like finger holes attached to the book.

Gabriel clapped and smiled as Dalton read.

While Gabriel was a blessing in Dalton's healing process, loud noises still terrified Dalton, and he would cover his ears with his hands.

Other times, he would say things like, "Mama and Daddy, I miss

Austin so much," or "When is the trumpet going to blow, so we can go to Heaven to see Austin?"

I know he missed his older brother, and as a result, he had an understandable fear of losing his younger brother. Many times, he asked, "Do I get to keep *this* brother forever?"

Nothing or no one would ever be able to fill the void of Austin, but I was so glad God allowed us to have Gabriel so Dalton could be a wonderful big brother to him.

As Gabriel grew, his energy level kicked into high gear. That boy had even more energy than Austin and *nothing would slow him down*. He ran from one end of our property to the other with our two dogs, a Basset Hound and a Corgi.

While the dogs nipped playfully at his heels, he chased Dalton around the yard, or his favorite thing, threw a football with Dalton or Jack.

At the age of two, Gabriel practiced singing, and, in my opinion, he sang like an angel. He wasn't afraid to sing in crowds. He loved singing everywhere he could: in church, in the car, and at the house. For Christmas, my parents and grandparents loved listening to him sing "Happy Birthday, Jesus."

One of Gabriel's favorite things was being a helper to my parents— his Grandma and Grandpa by setting his alarm and helping prepare meals for the holidays. He told me he felt it was *his* responsibility to help because they needed him. He drove our Polaris or walked the path to their house.

Even if it wasn't a holiday, he went to Grandma and Grandpa's house a few times a week to spend time with them and spin the fanciful tales that could come from a child's imagination. He reminded me of ny dad with his ability to capture all the details in a story. As he told stories, Gabriel would break out into a hearty laugh, much to the delight of my dad.

Even though the site of our family tragedy brought renewed sadness to my dad's heart, he never once neglected to honor Gabriel's wishes to ride the Polaris for a visit to the pond. As he'd done with Austin a multitude of times before, they fed the fish and even caught a few.

Gabriel was ecstatic to catch his first fish with my dad at the pond at the ripe age of three years old.

Even though Gabriel never had the pleasure of meeting Austin, we never hesitated to tell him everything about Austin when questions inevitably arose. It was our goal in life to assure that he felt as if he knew his oldest brother.

We told him stories of how Austin put on his videotape, singing and dancing, to "The Wiggles" with Dalton, and how he watched "Blues Clues" and carried around his handy dandy notebook along with his Bibles.

Austin was a very special boy, and we never wanted our boys to forget that.

In the spring of 2010, Jack and I were ecstatic to find out we were having *another* baby. Dalton was five years old, and Gabriel was two. The boys spoke to the baby inside my stomach and sang songs.

Life was so good! Jack and I prepared the baby room and gathered many boxes of diapers and other baby things. We announced the big surprise to our family, friends, and social media. Many family and friends were commenting about their excitement. They knew the life challenges we endured.

Everything was going very well until a few days before Easter. Our highs became lows as I developed complications with the pregnancy. The doctors didn't give much hope of the baby's survival, and for a week, the specialists had done all they could do to save the baby. The hormone levels rapidly declined, and I pleaded for the doctor's help.

I experienced too much loss for what I could handle. I couldn't take it anymore.

On Easter day, I had my *third* miscarriage.

When I came home, I crashed into my bed and wept like I hadn't done since the day Austin passed. This time, though, I felt the heavy grief of losing not one—but four—of my babies. *Four!*

I screamed out to God, "Why does this keep happening? Why have I lost *four* of my babies? Why do you keep taking them back to Heaven? I need them with me!" I screamed with an earnest plea, and I hit my bed with my fist.

I know it sounds crazy, and it is complicated to explain, but I heard God's voice with my natural ears. I didn't see Him, but I heard Him. His deep voice boomed as if he spoke through a microphone and spoke with authority—yet gentle at the same time. His voice was loud and clear, and he spoke so I understood every word. "Don't worry, my daughter. You will have a baby girl, and you will call her . . . Mikayla Ruth Haley."

It was shocking. I had chills on my arms, and I sat up in bed. I felt God relieve my fears and give me comfort. He gave me hope so I could have a reason to continue living. He gave me something *good* to dwell on.

It still wasn't easy, though.

The battle of having three miscarriages was beyond what this mom could endure, and I told God. I was honest with him. I wept, and I cried for those three babies and Austin to be with me. I cried night and day. But it didn't happen.

Some people may say it was "meant to be" or "They were meant to go to Heaven," but I don't like to think God would give those sweet babies to me to turn right back around and take them away. I couldn't take the thought, so I chose not to think that way.

Instead, I did my best to focus on the good things even though tears spilled over at the depth of my pain. I stayed focused as much as possible, so I didn't have a nervous breakdown, but I was desperate for help.

All three of my babies I lost to miscarriage went to Heaven and are now playing with Austin.

I liked envisioning their playtime in Heaven. *Austin is not alone.*

When Jack and I told the boys the baby died in my tummy, I don't think Gabriel understood as much as Dalton. Since Gabriel was two years old, he grieved but not as Dalton did. Dalton understood the finality of death since Austin's passing, and Dalton wept and cried as he laid down to sleep. He didn't understand why his brother or sister passed away, and his little heart was broken.

I put Dalton to bed, and I crawled under his blanket with him so that I could hold him close to me. We said our prayers, and we both wept together as he fell asleep in my arms.

God, please send peace. Please help us.

. . . Until We Meet Again

Those special memories of you will always bring a
smile

If only I could have you back for just a little while

Then we could sit and talk again

Just like we used to do

You always meant so much

And always will do too

The fact that you're no longer here

Will always cause me pain

But you're forever in my heart

Until we meet again

—Unknown Author—

Dalton's Visit to Heaven

Four months later, I woke Dalton up for school. "Good morning, my sweet Dalton," I whispered in his ear and kissed him on the cheek.

He laid there in silence for a few seconds without speaking. Finally, he managed to say in a drowsy whisper, "Mama, guess what, I got to see Austin last night. He took me to Heaven."

"Wh..wh..what? You had a dream of... Austin—in Heaven?"

"Yeah, do you want to hear it?"

"Absolutely! I wanna hear it all." I plopped on the edge of his bed, eager to hear every detail.

"Well, I was asleep in my bed, and I saw someone come through my ceiling. It didn't scare me, though. I heard someone saying in a quiet and sweet voice: Dalton, are you awake?

I was blinking my eyes to be able to see better in the dark and said "Yeah, who is it?"

"It's me, Austin—your bubba. I missed you, little brother, so I came to give you a hug and kiss."

"It felt so good to see my brother again!"

Dalton smiled as if he was remembering the dream in great detail. He had such a blissful look on his face. I sat next to Dalton on his bed and grasped my arms around my knee. My eyes filled with tears. I longed to hear *every* word he had to share with me. I couldn't wait to hear the entire story.

"What happened next, Son? Can you tell Mama?"

"Uh-huh. Austin stayed with me in my room for a little bit, and we played a few games. I wanted to play outside like when he still lived here, but I told Austin it was too dark.

Bubba said, "That's okay. Don't worry, little brother. We can go outside because God turns the night into day."

Austin snapped his fingers one time.

I was patiently waiting for Dalton's next words.

"Mama, you aren't going to believe it. It got so, so light outside—really, really fast!"

"How did you know it got light outside?"

"He showed me the light through my window when he pulled back the curtain, and we looked through the blinds. I couldn't believe it. It was light all of the sudden. How in the world did that happen? I wa amazed. He was like a superhero or something—better than Superman or Batman!"

"Wow, that's amazing. It must be a gift from Heaven to be able to turn night into day. So, what did you and Austin do next?"

"Bubba could tell I wanted to go outside to play so, so bad. That's where we always played together when he lived in our house. So, he helped me come up with a good plan. I liked his plan."

"Oh yeah? What was his plan?"

"Me and Bubba tiptoed by your bedroom, so we didn't wake you and Daddy up. After that, we went outside together. It was light out there, Mama. We were both so excited to see each other again!"

I smiled. "So, what did you do while you were outside in our yard?"

We laughed. We jumped. We ran, and we hugged a lot—a whole lot—in our front yard.

"Bubba was as happy as me. Then, we went to the backyard to play on the swing set. We ran as fast as superheroes could run. I could run as fast as him, too. Guess what?"

"What?" my eyes were now wide, sharing in his excitement. It seemed like old times again and hearing about conversations from when Austin was still with us. I couldn't wait to hear more details about their adventure together.

"We got to play chase again, and we even kicked a soccer ball for a while."

"Oh yeah, who won?"

Dalton giggled.

"We didn't keep score, Mama. It was just for fun. Lots and lots of fun."

Dalton sat up in bed. He began bouncing up and down on the mattress. I could tell his excitement was overflowing beyond what he could handle.

Dalton said, "Austin asked me if I wanted to go to Heaven with him for a while and see where he lives now. I was amazed, so I said, 'Sure!'"

"Oh, please, please tell me every detail, Son. I want to see what you saw! I'm dying to know every detail!"

"Ok. I'll tell you, Mama. This is what happened next. Austin grabbed my hand and took me to the front yard again. I couldn't believe we were together again. It felt so good for him to be with me. You won' believe what he showed me in our front yard.

"What was it?" My mind was racing with possibilities.

"There was a never-ever-ending staircase going up, up, up into the sky. Jesus came down from way up high.

"Wow, really? That's amazing. What did Jesus look like, Dalton?"

"Umm, he was wearing a shiny, white robe. It was super bright, and it was blowing in the wind. He had a red sash that went across like this."

Dalton gestured from his shoulder to his opposite hip.

"Wow, what did Jesus do when He saw you?"

"Well, he reached out His hand to me, so I took it."

"How did His hand feel? You held the hand of Jesus! Could you see the scars on his hand?"

"I'm not sure. I didn't notice.

"You didn't? Why not?"

"I couldn't stop looking into His eyes. He made my heart feel good Crazy good. Jesus made me smile because He loved me so much. could feel it right here."

Dalton patted his hand on his chest.

"Wow, it makes me want to cry, Son. I wish *I* could see Jesus face to face. I'd fall to my knees in worship. What did *you* do?"

"I was frozen. I couldn't move. It felt so perfect to see Him." Dalton's eyes stared out without a blink.

"I bet! What did you do next? I want to hear more."

"Jesus and Bubba walked with me up the staircase to Heaven. I thought we were going to walk a long, *long* time. There were tons of steps going super high."

For some reason, I giggled. "You were already tired from running and playing with Austin in the yard, weren't you? I bet those steps seemed like a huge mountain you were about to climb."

"Nooo, Mama, I was too excited to be tired. I was with Austin and Jesus!"

"Ah, I see," I replied with a smile, "So, what did the stairs look like?"

"They looked super shiny—like your jewelry."

"Ooh, that sounds pretty. What color were the steps?"

"They were silver, and they had gold on the sides. I only climbed three steps with Jesus because Heaven came fast."

"What? What do you mean, 'Heaven came fast?'"

"All of a sudden, I was just in Heaven!"

"Wait, you only walked up three steps? Then, you were in Heaven?" My mind was trying to remember every detail and not forget a single word.

"What did Heaven look like? Oh, my goodness, my heart is pounding! I can't believe you saw Heaven!"

"I did—I saw Heaven!"

"Oh, I believe you, Son. What did you see?"

"You'll never guess what's in Heaven and what it looks like Mama!"

"What? What's there? I can't wait to hear!"

"The grass was green—*super* green. There were flowers every where. In front of me, behind me, and under my feet. They smelled so good. I kept turning in circles, so I could see all of them. I've never smelled something so good before. It smelled so, so good!"

I sat in awe for his next few words. I could visualize every detail Dalton told me.

"All of the flowers were different colors. Lots and lots of colors— red, yellow, blue, pink. Mama, what is your favorite color?"

"Purple."

"Yep, God has your favorite color there, too."

"Wow, everything sounds so perfect in Heaven."

"It was so, *so* perfect. You have no idea! And guess what."

"What?"

"There were *beautiful* gates around Heaven."

"Gates?"

"Yeah, gates. Very, very pretty ones that sparkled. The walls were all different colors too. There were three gates around Heaven, and one was the *main* gate."

"Wait—slow down. Three gates and there was a *main* gate? How did you know it was the *main* gate?"

"Because Jesus told me."

"Tell me what the gates looked like. Please, Son. I want to know what it looks like there."

"Ok. They were gold gates with big, tall poles. A pearl was at the top of each pole. A *blue* pearl."

"How did you know it was a pearl?"

"I knew because Bubba told me. He pointed to it and told me the name."

I smiled at the thought of Austin still teaching Dalton, even though he was in Heaven. What a sweet boy Austin was—such an excellent big brother to him. He would want him to know everything about Heaven —no doubt.

"So, tell me more. What else did you see, Dalton?"

"Umm, there was a huge angel on each side of the main entrance. They weren't girls, though. They were boys. Both of them were holding big swords, Mama. And guess what?"

"What?"

"The swords were on fire! It was so cool! They kind of looked like the swords me and Bubba used to play with, but ours didn't have fire like theirs. They were much cooler than ours."

"That's so neat! Why do you think they had fire coming out of their swords?"

"I don't know." Dalton shook his head in wonder and shrugged his shoulders, "I think they were guarding Heaven, so only the people who loved Jesus could walk through. Me and Austin love Jesus a whole bunch, so we got to pass through the gate!"

"You are one blessed boy! Did the angels notice you at all? Did they say anything to you?"

"Yeah, they saw me, but they didn't talk to me. They were big but not bigger than me or Austin. We were big, too. The angels had on *very* white robes! It was amazing seeing Jesus *and* the angels! They wore gold over their white robes, too. It was on their shoulder and it went down like this." Again, he showed a motion from his shoulder to his opposite hip.

"Do you mean a *sash*—like Jesus was wearing?"

"Yeah, except the angels were wearing a gold one. It wasn't red like Jesus."

"Wow! So, what happened when you passed through the gate?"

Dalton reached up and touched his eyes and rubbed them. Then his eyes widened with excitement.

"My eyes! My eyes could see good all of the sudden! I could see everything I wanted to. My nose worked better, too. I could smell the flowers and the sweet smell of Heaven."

"So, Heaven smelled *sweet,* huh? I imagine it did!" I found myself smiling so big I couldn't contain it. I listened for his next word.

I noticed Dalton took his fingers and touched both ears at once. couldn't figure out what he was doing.

"Yeah, my ears could hear everything, too. It was much better than where we live on Earth. My ears could hear everything—all at once. But—it wasn't loud."

"What do you mean? What did you hear?"

"Birds were squeaking. Fish were jumping in and out of the water. Dalton started moving his arms in big arches like waves, going up and down. "I could hear the river, too. I could tell because my ears could hear all of it!"

Dalton stopped talking, and his eyes darted from side to side in his bedroom. I could tell he was reliving the amazing dream. He wa

emembering the sounds by the heavenly look that had appeared on his
ace.

I asked him, "When you were listening to the sounds, what was
Austin doing? I want to hear about him, too."

"Austin smiled because I liked it so much. He said, 'Hey, little
brother, let's go to the big swing set over there.'"

Dalton replied to Austin: "What? No way! Heaven has a *swing
set*?" Bubba nodded his head, "Yes." He grabbed my hand, and I
thought he was going to run with me, but we didn't have to. As soon as
he grabbed my hand and looked at the slide, we were there. We didn't
even have to walk. It was super awesome how fast we were there!"

"That's amazing you didn't have to walk, run, or anything! So, there
is a park in Heaven? Hmm. Wow, the Bible never tells us about that,
but there must be things there for the children to enjoy, I suppose."

"Oh, it's there! I saw it! We played on the swing that went up high
in the air."

"Wow, did it scare you to go that high?"

"Noooo, because nobody gets scared in Heaven, Mama."

I shook my head to show him I understood. "That's true. There's
nothing bad in Heaven, is there?" Thinking of the joy in Heaven made
me have goosebumps on my arms, and chills ran down my spine. What
else did you do in Heaven?"

"I saw Austin point to a giant winding slide that went around and
round and around with lots of colors. He asked me, 'Do you want to
ride on that?'"

"Yeah! That looks like so much fun. Come on!" I couldn't wait to
get there, so I grabbed Austin's hand, and I thought we were going to be
there immediately. But, I guess Austin wanted to run this time. I did

too. We laughed a lot. There were lots of kids there. It was such a fun playground."

"Oh, did you play with any of the other kids? Did you see any of your other brothers or sisters, by chance?"

"No, I wanted to spend all the time with my big brother."

"I understand that."

"Did you ever get on the big, winding slide?"

"Uh-huh, it was a *ton* of fun! There were buttons on the top of the slide. Yellow meant to go slow, red meant stop, and green meant to keep going."

"Oh yeah? That's so cool. Wow. How many times did you press the green button?"

"Oh, lots and lots of times. I couldn't stop—it was so much fun. But after a while, I sat at the top of the slide. I looked at Heaven. It was beautiful. So, so *beautiful*! I wanted to see more so bad, so I reached over and made myself push the red button. It was so hard to do that because it was so much fun."

"Wow, you must have seen so much of Heaven's beauty. What did it look like, Dalton? What else did you see when you got down from the slide?"

"Oh, man. It was so awesome. Austin walked me to the middle of Heaven. I couldn't believe what I saw!"

My heart was racing to hear more. "What? What was it? I can't even imagine."

"Right in the middle of Heaven was the *throne of God*," Dalton added, "There were hundreds and hundreds of angels singing."

"Wow, I bet their voices were so pretty. Did you know any of the songs they were singing? Do we sing them in church?"

"No, they weren't speaking English. It was in a different language, but their voices were perfect! Mama?

"Yes, Son?"

"The angels were worshiping God. The angels made God and Jesus smile when they sang. I loved it."

I smiled at the thought of the beauty that must have surrounded Dalton. "What did everything look like there in the middle of Heaven?"

"The room was gold, and the throne of God was too."

"Wait—you saw the throne? Did you see *God*?"

"Yeah, sort of. I couldn't see God's face, though. I tried to see Him, and I blinked a lot, but I couldn't."

"So, what did you see?" It looked like the sun was sitting on the throne; it was super bright. I don't know if I can explain the next part, Mama." His face creased, and his eyes narrowed in a look of concern.

"It's ok. Try to tell me what you can. I'll do my best to understand."

"Well, behind God was lots of colors. There were three swirling colors. Like a portal on TV, sort of."

"What colors were they?"

"Blue, purple, and pink."

"Hmm...I wonder what those colors mean in Heaven. Tell me more about God. Your dream seems so real—so true. I'm so amazed!"

"Oh, it was real! I was there! The throne that God sat in was a big, gold chair with those things that hold your arms."

"Armrests?"

"Yeah, armrests. The chair was huge, but it looked normal to us because we were also huge."

"Huge, huh? Wow! I still can't believe you saw the throne of God Dalton! You are very special to have this dream."

"I know. I felt special in Heaven."

"You are very, *very* special, my sweet son. God has plans for your future. What else did you see in Heaven? Please, tell me everything. Don't miss one single detail." I touched his cheek, lovingly. "What did it feel like there?"

"Umm, we could float. We weren't heavy at all."

"Wow, did you ever fly?"

"Sometimes. Most of the time, we didn't have to walk, run, or fly. We were just there."

"Wow, it sounds like such an amazing experience. What else did you see?"

"After that, Bubba asked me if I wanted to see another place. I was so excited. I screamed, 'Yes!' We didn't have to go very far because there was water Austin wanted to show me that was in front of God's feet.

"Water? What water?"

"It was called 'The River of Life'."

"Oh, my goodness. Are you serious? How did you know that was the name?"

"Austin told me. He told me everything about Heaven, and I'll never forget it. It had gold water, and we could see the fish because it was super clear. The fish jumped in and out of the water while they swam.

"Wow!"

"The water was calm, Mama. We watched the fish for a few

minutes. It reminded me of our pond, but it was much prettier than that."

"Amazing! What did the fish in Heaven look like?"

"They were colorful, and the fish jumped in and out of the water. It looked like they could fly. They almost floated."

"Wow! Did you ever go fishing with a fishing pole?"

"No, I wanted to swim with them."

"Oh yeah, did you get to?"

"Yeah, we got in the water and swam for a long time. It was amazing! Can you believe as soon as we got out, we were dry? We weren't even wet anymore!"

I smiled at the thought. "Immediately dry? That's awesome!"

"Yeah, it was very, very awesome! I can't believe we got to swim with the fish. I loved it! Do you want to hear more?"

"Of course, I do. Every single little detail."

"You'll never guess what else is in Heaven, Mama!"

"What? I can't believe you had such an amazing dream. Wow! What was it, Son? It brings Mama so much joy to hear your words."

"After we got done swimming, Austin pointed to a *beautiful tree*. I couldn't believe how *big* it was. It was much bigger than anything on Earth!

"Whoa, what did it look like?"

"It didn't just have *one* trunk. It had *two*!"

"What? Two? How did that work?"

"Yeah, one trunk was on the left side of the river, and the other trunk was on the other side.

"Wow, really?"

"Yeah, it came together at the top—above the river. It was a very tall tree. I remember feeling that the tree was *very* important."

"Important? Why?"

"I don't know. I guess because Bubba told me. He got serious—fast—and said, 'This tree is *very* important. Don't forget it, little brother. Tell everybody about it.' Austin looked at me very closely, and he wanted me to listen to his words.'"

"Wow, what he said next must have been very important. What did he tell you?"

Bubba asked me, 'Do you see me, little brother? Look at my body. I used to be hurt when I was on the fishing dock, but when Jesus brought me to Heaven, he brought me to this big, big tree.

"Do you see it way up there? Look at it. Do you see the leaves and how there is orange stuff dripping off of each one? You can see it right?"

"Mama, I looked way up there, and I stared at the leaves. I said, 'Yes, Bubba. I can see it.'"

"*That* is what healed me, little brother! It has medicine in the leaves. Do you see that I am okay now? I'm not hurt anymore. You don't have to worry anymore about me at all. I am okay now.

'This is the tree that heals everybody who is either hurt or sick, little brother. Don't forget the name—this tree is the most special one of all, and God calls it . . . 'The Tree of Life.'"

"Mama, it's *huge!* The tree is huge, and it's very special. *That tree healed Bubba!* I listened to what he told me. Bubba wanted to make me feel better, and it did. It made me feel lots better!

"I kept looking up to the tree. It was perfect, and I felt amazed. I couldn't stop looking at the orange stuff dripping from its leaves.

"So, *this* is what healed my big brother, Austin! I have never heard about the 'Tree of Life' before, Mama. I felt so thankful Austin showed it to me because, now, I don't have to worry about him anymore. My brother is *healed*, and he is in Heaven!"

I cried at that point—sobbed. The magnitude of the dream made oceans of tears fall from my eyes. I felt myself weaken and almost collapse on the bed. I knew this dream was God-given! I needed to hear every word, and somehow, Dalton was able to explain so many details. His words were soothing to my aching soul. Oh, how I missed my Austin—My Little Man.

Somehow, I felt I had seen the dream, too. My sweet Austin was healed and not in any pain. It caused joy to seep in through my heart and heal the broken cracks that were left from grief. God was mending my soul through my sweet boy's words. Oh, how I needed to hear every bit of his dream—every single word that escaped his lips.

Dalton continued his story as I sat silently with streaming tears. I couldn't say a word. My chin was quivering too much.

"Mama, Austin also showed me his big house. It sits on the biggest rock ever! It was such a big, beautiful house with many rooms inside of it."

Dalton somehow knew I needed to hear more without me telling him. I couldn't speak yet.

"I didn't notice as much on the inside. I was just amazed at how it sat on a huge rock. I liked it a lot."

I swallowed hard to make the huge lump in my throat go down. I managed to say, "His house sits on a huge rock, huh? Wow. It must be so beautiful in Heaven, Son."

"Yeah, so beautiful! I want to go back and see it all again."

"I would love to see it, too!" So, what happened after you saw his mansion?"

"My dream of Heaven ended."

"Wait—how did it end?"

"After we played in Heaven and I saw all of those things, I started getting sleepy. So, so sleepy. So, Jesus and Austin brought me back to my room and laid me in my bed. I told Austin, 'I'm sorry, Bubba, my eyes are starting to go closed. I'm getting sleepy now.' Austin leaned over and kissed me on the cheek.

"What did Austin say, Baby?" I asked.

Austin said, "That's okay. I've got to go back to Heaven to be with God and Jesus, but meet me in Heaven someday.'"

I looked him in his eyes, "Bubba, I promise, I will meet you in Heaven someday, and I will bring as many people with me as I can."

"After that, Mama, you woke me up. I tried to sit up, but my body felt heavy." I couldn't believe what just happened.

"I went to Heaven! I can't tell you how happy I am to see my brother again, Mama!"

I could tell Dalton felt better after he knew where his brother was and that he understood Austin was no longer hurt or in pain.

"Mama, he was my very best friend, and I need him. I can't wait to see Heaven and Austin again!"

By the time he had finished the story, I had tears dripping off my chin and I was shaking from head to toe. I knew he couldn't make this story up because Jack and I had taught him as much about Heaven as we could . . . about God, Jesus, the angels, the river, but we had never thought about mentioning the Tree of Life before! Dalton felt so special and loved by Austin that night.

Not too long after, he drew a picture of what he saw in Heaven that day, and I keep that in my Bible as a constant reminder . . . God has always taken care of us and always will take care of us. Thank you, God, for helping us through each and every day.

"Grief is like a tidal wave

Sometimes I'm able to ride it.

Sometimes it consumes me . . ."

—Unknown Author—

Physician Reports

One month after Dalton's dream, I was mopping the floor, and I began feeling nauseous. The feeling continued, lingering a few more days then worsened, so I went to the doctor. What I assumed was a virus, turned out to be something much different than I expected.

As I sat on the paper-lined bed in the examination room lost in a myriad of thoughts, I jumped when the doctor plowed into the room with a chart under his arm. They'd taken several blood samples and other diagnostic tests, so I steeled my gaze into his eyes as he walked in and slathered sanitizing foam onto his hands.

Did I have a common cold or maybe the beginnings of the flu? I didn't know, but I expected him to give me a dose of antibiotics and send me on my way. Instead, he floored me with these words: "Congratulations, Renee. You're going to be a Mama. Again," he said with a sly smile.

The room fell silent as the paper-lined table crunched under my shifting body. "Pregnant?" I whispered. Now the symptoms made perfect sense. "Why didn't this occur to me before now?"

He glanced at me with a knowing nod. "Blood doesn't lie. You're pregnant."

The doctor's report shocked me. We were expecting *another* baby!

A duality of emotions overcame me. I was excited yet scared, too. I had three previous miscarriages and couldn't bear the thought of another. Having experienced one broken heart after another, I'd become quite adept at the fine art of containing my feelings of excitement until we knew the baby's health was okay.

Dalton noticed I was nervous about the pregnancy.

One day, six weeks into the pregnancy as I studied the ultrasound photos in the living room, Dalton walked up to me and asked to hold the image of the ultrasound. I handed it to him, and he scrutinized it closely.

"Mama, she is a beautiful baby, and she will be born healthy and strong," he declared.

"Oh yeah? Do you think the baby is a girl?"

"I know she is! She will be so cute when she is born."

His confident words brought comfort to me, and the pregnancy continued with no complications.

Throughout the pregnancy, I taught at Noble Public Schools as I did with all my other pregnancies.

Tragedy

Given my history of miscarriages, Dr. Goff, an outstanding obstetrician, requested I keep weekly ultrasound appointments. We wanted to ensure nothing happened to this child in my womb.

Everything went well, and I could feel the baby's movements early in the pregnancy, which was a relief to Jack and me.

One month before the end of the school season, and eight months into my pregnancy, it was time for another ultrasound. Since the pregnancy had gone so well, and the doctor's office was thirty minutes away from my home, Dr. Goff allowed me to make the decision whether or not I wanted to cancel the ultrasound appointment.

I thought about canceling, but I wanted to see the baby as much as possible on the monitor, so I traveled to Mercy Hospital in Oklahoma City, Oklahoma, for my final ultrasound.

As the sonographer began the ultrasound scan, we visited about my amazing school day and other benign topics. His happy smile vanished from his face, and he stopped talking mid-sentence.

His expression had transitioned from cheery and pleasant to being clouded with worry and darkness, and I felt the blood drain from my face. "Is—is everything okay with the baby?" I whispered, tension crept into my voice as I sent up silent prayers that everything was fine. Surely, we weren't this far into the pregnancy only to face yet another unthinkable situation.

The technician looked at me with eyes of concern and compassion. "There's almost no amniotic fluid around your baby, and the baby isn't responding as much as we'd like at this time, although the heart is still beating."

"*What?* Oh no. This can't be. No!"

The technician placed his hand on my forearm in a gesture of reas suring support. "Have you felt the baby move in a while?"

I scrambled to recall the last time I'd felt movement. "Yes, I noticed movement while I was in front of my class teaching this morning and also throughout the afternoon."

"You didn't feel any changes at all throughout the day?"

Changes? What kind of changes? I'd had no pain or otherwise strange sensations that would lead me to think something was wrong No leakage of any kind. "Everything has been normal."

I lay in silent angst as he continued the ultrasound for a few more agonizing minutes, but the look on his face grew continued signs o concern.

I knew that look all too well, and although I tried to relax, fea swept my mind. *No, God, don't take another baby. I can't handle i again! Please, keep this baby safe.*

The room became silent as the sonographer took a few more scans "Your baby is in acute distress without an adequate amount of amniotic fluid, so your doctor will want you to drive to labor and delivery They'll put you on intravenous drips and monitor your baby."

I walked to the car in a daze and barely registered the hum of daily activities going on around me, but the clarity of mind made it through the mental haze and told me I had to get to the hospital as fast as could. The safety of my baby, of *our* baby, depended on it.

When I arrived at the Labor and Delivery Unit, I hoped they would tell me everything looked fine, but their assessment aligned with that of the sonographer. There was a low amount of amniotic fluid and the baby was in distress.

"You need to prepare to induce in a few hours if fluids don' ncrease with this IV, okay?" A nurse told me in a measured voice of assurance.

"But, I'm still five weeks away from the due date. Will the baby be born healthy?"

"The baby should be fine, but we can't be certain. At this point in the pregnancy, a few days can make a huge difference in the baby's growth and health, so we need to wait as long as we can before delivering."

When the nurse left the room, I called Jack, who was as worried and shocked about the news as I was.

In the event the baby would arrive earlier than anticipated, he returned home and packed our hospital bags, put together the car seat, and finalized all the last-minute details.

Even though the hospital staff had done all they could do, the amniotic fluid wasn't increasing to the volume needed to assure the baby's safety, so they prepared to induce delivery within the next few days. They gave me steroid shots to help the baby be stronger after birth.

At 8:00 a.m. on April 25, 2011, two days after the sonogram, my water broke, and the doctors gave me Pitocin through my IV to begin the labor process. However, little progression continued throughout the day, so he stopped the IV from running through the night and began it again the next morning at 10:30 a.m.

The labor progressed as expected throughout the day, and at 8:05 p.m. on April 26, 2011, Jack and I welcomed our first baby *girl*. She was beautiful but very small. Our daughter, Mikayla Ruth Haley, was five pounds three ounces and eighteen and a half inches long. We were happy to report to our family and friends that she was born healthy without a single issue that is often linked with such a premature birth.

When Dalton, now six-years-old, held her for the first time at the hospital, he said, "I love Mikayla so much, and she is *so* beautiful—more beautiful than me."

Gabriel, almost three years old, responded, "I love her, too! Even more than my Nintendo."

Jack and I were proud parents of a baby girl, and she blessed our family so much. Dalton and Gabriel adored her, gave her a constant flow of hugs and kisses, and told her how much they loved her.

We dressed her in pink frilly dresses and enjoyed having a *girl* in our home for the first time. We decorated her room with pink and purple butterflies.

As Mikayla grew older, we began to see how much she resembled her oldest brother, Austin.

She had brown hair and light brown eyes just like him, though he had darker brown eyes. It surprised us to see just how much she favored him. Mikayla was such a blessing.

Dalton, Gabriel, and Mikayla were a dynamic team in making things fun around the house. It was nice to see all three of them running and playing together around the yard, on the swings, in the sandbox, and on the trampoline.

They developed a special bond and enjoyed activities together such as playing basketball in the backyard. Most of the time, Mikayla used a toy whistle, so she could be the referee while the boys played one-on-one. Jack and I would sometimes join in on the fun for a game or two as well, which delighted them.

Life became fun with our three children, but none of our three children ever replaced Austin. We still longed to see him again and wished he could be part of the daily family fun.

My dad was beyond thankful to see Gabriel and Mikayla born, but he had become weaker and very ill with Hepatitis C.

"Jack, a person only lives about twenty years with Hepatitis C. You've had it now for thirty," the doctor told him one day at a checkup. "I don't know how you have survived it these many years, but your liver can't take much more because your enzymes are extremely elevated."

"I know, Dr. Wright. God has blessed me with years beyond what I thought I would have. My grandson, Austin, prayed for me four years ago, and God must be answering his prayers. God must want to keep me around a while longer."

"Yes, you've been given extra time beyond what most people get, but the cirrhosis in your liver is beyond what you can handle much longer."

"I know, Doctor. I know I don't have much time left. I've had a good life, but there is so much I still want to do with my wife, kids, and grandkids."

Dr. Wright was part of a team of doctors who *invented* the medical cure for Hepatitis C, and a few years later, my dad took the treatment and was cured of the Hepatitis C virus.

My dad was one of the first people in the United States to successfully overcome the terrible virus. In my opinion, these things don't happen by accident. It was *seven years* by the time all of Austin's prayers were answered, but all of them eventually were. We are beyond thankful for the good things God has done for our family.

My dad was cured of Hepatitis C thirty-three years after his blood transfusion following the terrible oil rig explosion. His healing didn't come to pass for a long seven years, but we always kept our faith that God would make a way, and He did.

"It takes strength to make your way through grief, to grab hold of life and let it pull you forward."

—Patti Davis—

Until the Battle is Over

Until we see Austin again, life continues. Jack and I have had excellent times with our other children, and we feel blessed to be their parents.

Dalton is now seventeen years old and a junior in high school. When he was younger, struggling with Austin's death, Jack and I placed him in Taekwondo to help him through the pain of enduring the loss of his big brother.

He became a second-degree black belt and went to World Championships when he was six years old and received second in sparring and third in his form. Without a doubt the sport helped to motivate him, giving him the courage to face obstacles in life.

ATA Taekwondo Magazine published our story about Austin, and the article recognized Dalton's faith and courage for continuing with life after such a tragedy.

Dalton is tall in stature at six feet seven inches, and he is on a mission to help others by changing the world one person at a time. Once he graduates high school in the year 2023, he plans to enroll in a Doctorate of Psychology program, so he can help others who have also faced traumatic situations in life.

Right now, though, his primary interest is reading and studying the Bible. He researches different religions daily and is ready to witness to others at any time.

As I watch the young man Dalton has become, my mind can't help but swell with pride as I recall the witness he is to everyone around him. A few months ago, he rode the school bus to a sporting event when the bus driver overheard him speaking about God to one of the other students.

The bus driver contacted me later and said, "I need to tell you that Dalton spoke with knowledge, compassion, and wisdom to his friend. It inspired me to see a sixteen-year-old speak so boldly about Jesus. Dalton's words caught my attention and had an impact on my life."

Not too long after Austin's passing, I prayed that Dalton and our future children would have their *own* blessings in life as well as the blessings *Austin* would've had. I believe with all my heart God answered that prayer.

One of Dalton's goals is to become valedictorian of Noble High School's Class of 2023. He said, "I know Austin would have been valedictorian because he was intelligent and could read at such a young age so it is my goal to not only become valedictorian for myself but also for Austin since he never had the opportunity."

Dalton has always made straight A's in school and has received high honors in his classes. He has been taking college classes while finishing his high school degree. He will be a sophomore in college by the time he graduates high school.

He also excels as a musician. As a trumpet player, he has received state awards. His natural expertise as a musician is also evident in that he taught himself how to play the piano, guitar, and bass. He has been invited to play TAPS at the funerals of several Veterans.

For him, music serves as a form of therapy because it helps him cope with the loss of Austin.

I'm happy to report that Dalton is doing very well emotionally since Austin's tragedy. He enjoys having a good time and making people laugh.

I also see in him a great leader in life, and people enjoy being around him.

Gabriel is now fourteen years old and is six feet three inches tall and is about to begin his first year of high school. He plays the saxophone and works very hard in school. God has blessed him with the ability to make straight A's since kindergarten, and he's achieved several high honor awards.

He has a hearty laugh, is kind-hearted, compassionate, and cares for his family and friends. People enjoy spending time with him.

Like his siblings, he enjoys attending church with the family and the youth group at the church where we have attended for the last three years.

Detail-oriented, just like his brother, Austin, Gabriel can easily recall information stored in his memory.

As of now, he wants to become a defense attorney. My dad taught him as much as he could throughout the years, so I believe he could be successful in the law profession someday.

Gabriel is a mighty blessing in our family because he helped us carry a smile once again.

Mikayla is eleven years old, five feet and three inches tall, and has long brown hair and brown eyes. Like her brothers, she also works hard in school and has made all A's in her classes.

She enjoys playing basketball and soccer and often takes rides in the Polaris with me, and we feed the fish at the pond. Her laugh rolls over the pasture as she watches the fish, especially when the splash of waves soak her from head to toe.

Jumping on the trampoline or petting the cat in Jack's shop are some of her favorite pastimes, and like most girls, she loves spending time with friends, chasing her brothers around the house, or playing card games like Uno on the living room floor.

She has become quite a great artist, drawing with expertise. She also enjoys watching Netflix movies with the family, loves hearing about Jesus, and often reads stories in her Bible.

What a blessing she is to us!

f Austin was still living, he would have graduated from Noble High School with the Class of 2020.

When the time of his graduation rolled around, it was another sad moment for our family because Austin wasn't there to enjoy all the senior events that kids his age anticipate. All the main milestones in life are difficult to see come and go, but we were thankful to attend several of his senior events.

In August 2020, the seniors painted the senior parking lot with an image of their choice. Seth, one of Austin's best friends, chose to paint his spot with a camouflaged football. It represented Austin saying, "Now, I'm in the Lord's Army." Around the painted football on the asphalt, it was Austin's favorite verse—Jeremiah 17:7.

The painting matched the shirts he and his friends wore when they were six years old and came to our house to release balloons on Austin's sixth birthday.

Other friends painted Austin's name, his football jersey number 23, or his favorite verse. It was very special and made us feel blessed that his friends still remembered him twelve years later.

In November 2020, Dalton again woke up telling me about a dream he had.

"Mama, I dreamed Austin was at the Senior Send-Off Football Game that is happening this evening."

"Really? I'm glad you had another dream of him. It's so sad Austin won't be there. I sure wish he could've been here for his senior year."

"Me too. I thought it was interesting in my dream, how he walked out with a gold uniform, but all the others on the team dressed in blue. The gold reminded me of him coming from Heaven. He stood between two of his best friends, Carson and Seth."

Later that afternoon, Seth's mom, Amy, called me to ask if we could attend the Senior Send-Off Football Game that evening because they had something to present to us.

Even though I felt sad about Austin not being there to participate, was happy for Austin's friends. As the football players walked onto the field for the Senior Send-Off to take pictures and begin the ceremony we were shocked to see the football team dressed in blue with his two best friends holding a *gold* jersey with Austin's number, twenty-three emblazoned across it.

I glanced over at Dalton. "This reminds me of what you saw in your dream."

"Yes, I can't believe it. It's what I saw."

The players lined up to prepare for the pregame coin toss with their backs to the stands so we could see the number on the backs of their erseys. They stretched Austin's gold jersey between his two best friends.

We all rushed to take photos with our cell phones, and my sister-in-law, Ericka, approached to show me the picture she took.

"Renee, look at this photo," she said. "I have no idea how it happened because it is unedited, but there is a ray of light shining down on Austin's gold jersey and Austin's two best friends."

The picture astonished me. In my mind, it was a perfect representation of the ray of light streaming down from Heaven, received at a time we needed it the most. It seemed Austin was near and shining down on us.

The football team presented us with a ceramic doll that parents painted for their athletes. The football moms worked hard to make us one as well. It had brown hair and brown eyes to represent Austin. On his shoes, they painted the words, "Jeremiah 17:7" for his favorite verse.

A few days before Austin's graduation I wrote the following thoughts on my Facebook page: "Your friends picked up their caps and gowns today, and I am so happy for them. They have achieved great things! They have worked more years for this diploma than any others they will receive in the future.

Soon, they will reunite once again for graduation. Everyone now must distance themselves because of COVID. Our family has "distanced" since 2007 when you went to be with Jesus.

What would it have been like for you to attend your graduation, Austin? We had dreams for your future. Would you have been the class Valedictorian and worn the gold sash around your neck? Would you have carried any honors or awards such as All-State? What would your future occupation have been? What would you have become? What would your life have held?

As Mother's Day and graduation approach, I am reminded of our sweet five years, nine months, and ten days together. You made me proud! I wish you were here with me, enjoying these special moments. You should have been a graduate of 2020 from Noble High School. I should have seen you walk across that stage.

But, I must remember, you *did* graduate . . . when you went to Heaven. You haven't missed out. You received the biggest award of them all when your name was called from the King of Kings and Lord of Lords, "*Welcome home, Austin Gabriel Haley*," and you were issued a new name. Your graduation cap was a *crown* with many stars in it, I am sure since you witnessed to so many.

Rather than a robe of Noble blue, you had a robe of sparkly white. Rather than a diploma, you received a mansion. Oh, I can envision that smile on your face as you received these things after "walking the stage" into Heaven's open gates and sitting at the feet of Jesus and studying His face. Oh, how perfect it must be.

As I think about the past on earth, your present and future plans were to be in the Lord's army, and you wanted the whole world to come to know Jesus. Your eyes were always set on heavenly things.

Someday, my precious son, I will join you there, and I pray others make the decision to live for Jesus as well, but for now, I'll keep you in my heart always and forever as I work along with you in the Lord's army, trying to spread the name of Jesus so the whole world will come to know Him. Austin, you may have started the race, but I'm doing my best to continue the amazing race you have begun.

Since Austin's graduation took place during the difficult COVID year, the school administration decided that each graduate walk across the stage while their families drove past the stage in their vehicle.

Even though Austin couldn't be in attendance, they honored him by calling his name, followed by a moment of silence. We decorated the windows of the car, "In Memory of Austin Haley—Class of 2020," along with his favorite Bible verse. What a blessing it was for Noble Public Schools to recognize our son, Austin. I will never forget the support we have received.

"Your memory lives forever in my heart as I continue on the path life set before me."

—Amy Hoover—

When the Storms Come

My dad, the one who took Austin fishing that day, passed away from Sudden Cardiac Arrest in May 2021.

We continued our ride to the pond all of these years to let my other children feed the fish and enjoy the same things Austin did.

I'm going to miss him with all of my heart. The pond is much quieter now that I don't hear my dad's voice, happiness, and laughter, but I will continue making the trip in his Polaris to remember him. His love will remain in my heart forever.

For now, he is reunited with Austin in Heaven, and I am on a mission to finish this test I call "life" so I can see both of them once again in Heaven.

When life is testing, and I cannot bear any more pain or heartache, God gives me something good in my life. He will never put more on me than I can handle, and I place my trust in Him. God cares for me, and He loves me.

Life is full of struggles. Whatever my struggle through life, I will do my best to remember God will carry me through.

When things seem difficult, I'll find the good things and think about them. I may not understand why I have to go through life's disappointments, but I rest in God's presence. God is in control.

There are times in life I may think, *what have I done to deserve this?* But, I will keep the faith and believe God will help me. God is merciful, and His presence is with me until the end.

The waves of grief may crash around me. The storm is real, but stand firm with God on my side.

Since the loss of my son, losing my dad was one of the most difficult things I had to face in life, but I am reminded that . . . *God is faithful!* look back over our lives, and I have witnessed it. I have lived it – my dad was a wonderful example of it.

My mom and dad met through her brother, Mike, who also happened to be my dad's best friend. Mike agreed to be their best man but just a few months prior to their wedding he was tragically killed in a car accident. *But God was faithful!* My mom and dad were blessed in their marriage and celebrated their 50th anniversary in November 2020.

When my sister was two and my mom was six months pregnant with me, we were in a rollover accident. My sister and mom were ejected forty feet from the car, but *God was faithful!* My dad also survived the wreck and held my mom's and sister's hands in that hot field and prayed out to God. He declared everything would be ok since he had talked to God and no doctor could tell him differently. My mom carried me full term! My sister had a severe head injury, but God miraculously healed her two weeks later in church.

Two months after I was born, our home burned down, but *God was faithful!* My mom, my sister, and I all made it out alive. Friends, people, and even strangers helped us in our time of need.

In 1981, my dad went on his first day to the job in the oil field. There was a terrible explosion that almost took my dad's life. It changed his life forever, but *God was faithful!* As my dad lay on the ground, he asked God for life and asked that he be allowed to raise his children. My dad asked for twenty more years, but God gave him forty (almost to the day)! He was able to meet each grandchild, including the newest unexpected surprise—my brother and sister-in-law's baby, Caroline! My dad returned to college after the accident and earned his law degree to be able to help others, too. We have heard of many people who loved my dad and appreciated his guidance and help in times of need.

In 2007, my dad witnessed the tragic death of Austin. This was so hard on him and the entire family, *but God was faithful!* God honored a prayer prayed by Austin the night before he passed away and blessed our family with two additional children, Gabriel and Mikayla. Many people have come to know Jesus through Austin's story, and we are so thankful there are good things to think about. There is no doubt my dad is with Austin now!

Over the years my dad had many health issues—allergic reactions to insulin and beef, multiple heart attacks, multiple strokes, staph infections (one in his heart), Hepatitis C for thirty-five years from his accident, diabetes, pneumonia, etc. The list could go on and on, but *God was faithful!* God healed my dad more times than I can count. We often said he had more than nine lives. The fact is that God granted our prayers many times. He has never left us or forsaken us. He's walked with us, or carried us if necessary, through every situation.

On May 24, 2021, my dad went to see Jesus, and *God is faithful!* My dad had told us he wanted to pass away at home. He didn't want to be in the hospital or nursing home. He didn't want to linger or be a burden. God granted my dad's desires. His heart stopped beating in the living room near his chair. He went from this life to a life in Heaven. No more of his old worn-out physical body. He now enjoys his new heavenly body. He's waiting for us there, and I plan to see him again one day.

Even though I have gone through a difficult time with Austin's death, I choose to think back to all the times that God has been faithful. He's always there guiding, making a way, and answering prayers. God has sustained me. He has blessed me and has met my needs.

Tragedy

My dad's headstone says he lived from 1949-2021. The years don't matter . . . what matters is what my dad did with his life during the dash (-) between the years. It's what defined him and what we'll remember about him. My dad was gentle-hearted and affectionate. We never doubted his love for us—he said it! He loved God with all his heart, was a praying man, and taught God's Word to others. He's received his reward. The rest of us have work left to do and life left to live! It's what we do with the dash that counts. No doubt . . . *God will continue to be faithful!*

For fourteen years, I have searched for Austin's fishing pole he used on the day he passed away on August 3, 2007.

Two weeks before my dad passed in May 2021, I rode on the Polaris with my dad. I told him how much I would like to locate Austin's fishing pole he used that day. We knew it landed in the water, and it was in the pond somewhere.

I asked my dad to describe it if he could. He told me, "Oh, Honey, it's been too long, and I don't remember." He got silent for a few seconds and continued, "If I remember, though, it was black with red lines going up the pole."

I didn't think about it anymore until a few days after my dad passed.

I was mowing the embankment that went to the fishing dock, the same hill I mowed many, many times the past fourteen years.

My mower hit something hard. When I took a closer look, it was the handle of a fishing pole. I dug the fishing pole out of the mud at the bottom of the embankment, and the black fishing pole had red lines going up the pole.

I got on social media on a group that evaluates old fishing poles. I posted photos of the pole, but I didn't explain anything. I asked about the year and brand of the fishing pole.

They told me the type and said, "This fishing pole was from the early 2000s, and it would be perfect for a young child who is learning how to fish."

They didn't know my story about Austin, but it gave me the answer I needed.

Was it a coincidence? Maybe or maybe not. But the fishing pole was most likely the one Austin was using fourteen years ago.

The fishing pole is now sitting next to Austin's curio cabinet. His curio cabinet is filled with many of his favorite items: his camouflage Bible, his bear blanket, Transformers, puzzles, sports equipment, and more. The curio cabinet holds a special place in our hearts, so it sits in our living room where we can be near Austin's favorite belongings.

"We bereaved are not alone. We belong to the largest company in all the world—the company of those who have known suffering."

—Helen Keller—

For the Grieving Heart

I want to speak to those who are broken-hearted today. This type of pain is excruciating and is more than many of us can handle at times. The loss of a child, a close loved one, or other traumatic event changes the life we all once had. It's not fair at all.

As you encounter your own life problems, you may find yourself without hope or desire to live, but I encourage you to remember the sage advice of Philippians 4:8. 'Finally, brethren, whatsoever things are true, whatsoever things are honorable, whatsoever things are just, whatsoever things are pure, whatsoever things are lovely, whatsoever things are of good report, if there be any virtue, if there be any praise, think on these things.'

When your mind is burdened with negative thoughts, make a conscious effort to infuse your mind with good things instead. When you do, it may not completely take the pain away, but it will lift your spirits and bring you through difficult times. Despite your tremendous pain and heartache, endeavor to stay focused on what brings peace of mind rather than what brings pain.

You can make it through the lonely, dark hours you're facing. It may feel as though you are sinking, but find hope in life! Find comfort in God, family, or a trustworthy friend who can help you through.

No, we don't understand why bad things happen, but they do. Please, don't lose faith and hope. You can make it through the difficult times of life.

To help you through the turbulent waters of grief, I have compiled a few suggestions that helped my family along the way, and I hope they may help you as well.

First, in the midst of your pain—yes, even through tears and heartache—find someone else who needs encouragement today. Your tears and your story may help *them*. Sometimes, you may not even have to say anything at all. Just listening to their story and being a solid presence in their life may be all they need. In short, we must be there for each other.

Second, if you're grieving a loss, stop and remember something good your sweet child or loved one *did*. What did they love? What brought joy into their life? Was it giving someone a tight hug or going somewhere that was special to them? (Our sweet Austin loved going to the pond). Maybe it could be something as simple as reading their favorite book, watching a television show or movie they enjoyed, or listening to their favorite song. Whatever that looks like, find a way to do one good thing your loved one did. Do it with intention—to bring happiness back into your life.

Do it in memory of those whom you love. Yes, you may cry, and that's okay. It's important to allow yourself the opportunity to navigate through the often-treacherous ebb and flow of the grieving process. Tears are a language we all speak, and they serve an incredible purpose in healing a broken heart.

Also, maybe it would help you to create a symbol that represents the person you long to see. What I mean is, think about what they loved, their passion, and their happiness. Some of you may think about a verse in the Bible, a horse, a tree, a flower, a number they wore in sports, etc. Whatever you decide on, post the symbol in your bedroom, on your social media page, or in your front yard—wherever you can maintain easy visual contact with it. It may seem like a small thing, but you'd be surprised how it helps bring your loved one back to your thoughts through the tedium of your day.

I don't want to impart false hope that you'll ever "get over" the loss of the person you love, because you won't, but with time it will get a little easier. In the meantime, always remember them, continue loving them, and think about them often.

Another thing I did that might be helpful to you: rather than feeling the emptiness in your heart when going through the motions of "boxing up" the treasures, they left behind, how about displaying them in a curio cabinet or on a shelf? It could make you feel as though they are still with you in a special way. Rather than discarding their earthly treasures or shoving them in a closet in an "out of sight, out of mind" manner, embrace their treasures by adopting them into your own home. Allow the patina of love they left in their belongings to carry you through the bad days. It's a wonderful tribute to their life.

Keep in mind that it's impossible to verbalize to anyone how deep your pain runs. Regardless of their best intentions, nobody understands what you've been through.

I don't know what you face in your life right now, and if I did, I wouldn't know what to say. People rarely know what to say to help, but God does.

He sees you right now, and He knows what every tear represents as they fill your eyes and drip down your face.

Some of you reading these words right now have tried in vain to find a ray of hope through the storm you have tread. You have tried to find a reason to live. If you take one thing away from our story, please let it be that God is your only *true* hope. Think on good things.

To this day, I still don't understand everything about forgiveness, but I do feel much better after forgiving the police officers.

If applicable in your situation, if you can find the heart to forgive, please take every step to do so as soon as possible, as the chains of unforgiveness are heavy and will impede, not help, your journey to true healing. Forgiveness helps take away some of the burdens and lighten the load of heartache and pain.

It may be useful to think of giving the burden, the injustice, to God to handle on your behalf. It brings unexplainable peace. In your mind visualize the person you need to forgive. Whether they ask for your forgiveness or not, begin forgiving them today. Forgiving someone is not a one-time event. It may take days, weeks, or months even. You may have to forgive them every time you think of them, but it will bring you peace as you have never felt.

Tragedy

You can make it through your pain and come out on the other side a healthy, happy, and healed person. It won't be easy and taking the first step to forgiveness is the hardest, but for now, put one foot in front of the other and decide in your heart what you'll do. Take it one second, one minute, one hour, and eventually one day at a time. You *can* make it.

You will smile without the grief, heartache, and agony you feel now. Stay focused on good things—do it with intention, so that you can be lifted out of despair.

You can make it! Remember, you are not alone.

"May the peace that comes from the memories of love shared, comfort you now and in the days ahead."

—Unknown Author—

Reflection on the Pond

It was a blissful evening. The sun peeked through the branches of the trees, glistening across the dock with its warmth enveloping me. I sat down on the dock and watched as the ripples of water moved. Then I leaned over the side and made a circle in the pond with my index finger in thoughtful contemplation.

I spent a moment by myself at the pond. I could hear the chirping of the birds, the footsteps of deer prancing through the field, and the gentle rustling of leaves in the trees. Other than that, it was silent.

My heart felt much lighter, and I wasn't angry with the noises of nature anymore. I rolled to my back. First I closed my eyes and enjoyed the sounds. Then, looking straight up to the heavens, I saw the clouds shifting. I remembered all the times I'd spent with Austin. Just like the clouds moved and changed, so did life.

It seemed I lived two lives now. The life with Austin and the one after he passed.

I couldn't help but think back.

I reflected on the moment when Austin passed away and the events that followed. How often is it that a child has knowledge of their upcoming death? It seems a very unusual thing that people know what is about to occur.

Austin began having nightmares that police officers were going to take him away from us when he was three years old, and they continued until the morning before his death.

When Austin was having the premonitions, we thought they were only bad dreams. We didn't know he was going to die. However, Jack and I cringed at the thought of losing our child when Austin recounted his stories. I wouldn't allow my mind to go there, and I pushed it away while turning our focus on comforting Austin.

There were several things I still didn't understand: Why did Austin have those nightmares? What purpose did it serve him to know this. Why didn't God just take him and not forewarn him?

Many people have told me it must have been God preparing him for Heaven. Maybe that's true. I like to believe so.

I became curious about other children around the world who had premonitions of their own death. I looked it up on the internet and social media. I even joined groups for grieving parents, and I asked them if their children had the same experiences. Several of them did but I found out that every situation was different.

Most people were older, not the age of five.

Tragedy

With all of the studying and research I had done on the topic of a child having knowledge of their upcoming death, I had found the answer, nobody knows why, but it does happen from time to time—more often than most people realize.

God knew. He had knowledge that moment was coming with Austin's death. But, if he let Austin know through nightmares, why didn't God allow *me* to know? Why didn't he tell or warn *me*?

But, it would have been much too difficult for my mind to bear.

That's why I leave it in God's hands. I don't have all the answers.

I sat up on the wooden dock that stood alone behind the trees. A gentle breeze swept my hair behind me, and the trees spoke with a whistle or two to remind me I was not alone. On the dock, it felt undisturbed, peaceful. But, my mind still raced with thoughts from before.

Why didn't the police check what was behind their target? I still didn't understand. Their training should've prevented such a mistake. My little boy would still be here.

I pictured all of my children, together, running here and there, making paths through the trees, and bursting out with laughter. That's the way life should've been.

But, life, as I expected, was changed by a narrow moment of time—one almost uncountable. Six seconds from the first *BOOM* to the next. That's all it took for everything to be different. It still took my breath away to hear the *BOOM* in my thoughts, and I cringed at the loud, powerful blast in my ears.

Many people asked the reason for not suing the Police Department or the policeman who made the fatal shot. Some suspected it was for religious or financial reasons. But, it wasn't that. We were just plum exhausted and in too much pain.

I'm sure we could've sued the Police Department for reckless decision-making that resulted in the death of our sweet son, but we couldn' wrap our minds around it long enough to sustain court again. Also, the people who lived in Noble were our friends. It is where I had lived since I was in second grade. It didn't feel right. Maybe we made the right decision or maybe not.

I stood up and reached in the metal bucket for fish food and threw in a few pieces. Outward ripples of circles appeared on the calm water reminding me of the circle of life. We are all born, and we are all going to die someday. Austin's circle was five years, nine months, and ten days. We never know how much life we have left to live.

How do *I* want to spend my time?

There was a heavy pause in my movements as I looked at my own reflection in the water. I stood in silent, deep contemplation.

Sometimes, life brings disappointments, struggles, and pain. Most of it, I will never understand. The pain goes deeper than words could express. I planned to use that pain to help others cope with their *own* grief—somehow, someway.

Tears began to flow down my cheeks, not from my own pain this time but from others. The burden I carried was for others who had faced the grief of their own.

I imagined myself walking up to them, wrapping my arms around their neck, and whispering, "You can make it. Whatever you are going through, you can make it! Keep pressing forward one step at a time. Sometimes, the steps will be slow and weary, feeling like quicksand is gripping you to the core, but keep moving. Stay focused for that finish line of life. Do you see it in view? Life is a race you must win. Keep pressing toward that finish line, and you will see your loved ones again.

Tragedy

I trudged back up the hill and turned around to see the dock from a distance. The leaves crunched under my feet, and I watched as the limbs appeared to be waving at me. Whatever life brings, I will lean on God, stay close to Him, and trust in Him with each step I take. God's plan will be mine.

A WORD FROM AUSTIN'S DAD AND GRANDPARENTS

A Father's Memories

WRITTEN BY JACK HALEY

Losing my five-year-old son was difficult to endure and still is. I needed God's help. God gave me a family, and I felt it was my duty to take care of them.

It was hard seeing Austin pass from my life. Our family was never the same again. To endure the thought of not having the entire family together anymore was more than I could handle. Our family would never be complete again—we would always be missing one child. I needed God's help to endure such heartache.

Losing Austin was *not* the first time I endured loss. My mom went through an unthinkable tragedy, losing a son (my brother, Daniel

Haley) and her husband (my dad, Floyd Haley) in May of 1975; I was almost five years old.

A semi-tractor and trailer lost control on a bridge. My dad drove a truck with a trailer and hauled a John Deere tractor. The semi jack knifed, and there was no place for my dad to get out of the situation. My brother was killed instantly, while my dad lived a short while.

My mom's life was turned upside down. She was a housewife who had lost the love of her life. She didn't know how to drive, and she had to find a job to support her children. Life was not easy for her.

Since the accident, the Haley family has grown, and there are many grandchildren and great-grandchildren. We have come a long way, but our family will always miss my dad and brother.

My mom is the reason for our family being close-knit. She carried faith, strength, and courage to continue raising her children. After the tragedy of losing her husband and son, she had eight children at home to care for and provide for. Since she never remarried, I know it wasn't easy. She had to do it all alone.

I never mourned the death of my dad or brother until I lost my son. I grew up without a dad, so I didn't know how having a dad was supposed to be.

Losing Austin, my dad, and my brother was too much for me.

Little did I know of the surprise and finality that bullet would have on our family that terrible day.

I had spent four years in the military (United States Air Force) which gave me a lifetime perspective of discipline, leadership, and protection. I have been an aircraft crew chief in charge of the safety of a fighter aircraft and the well-being of the crew that flew it.

I have been involved in the maintenance and restoration of aircraft or thirty-two years now; twenty of those years, I was an aircraft nspector at Tinker Air Force Base. With that in mind, discipline, leadership, and protection are valuable to me.

I was always protective of Austin. I would make sure his hand was held by either me or Mama while crossing the street. We didn't leave his side when we were in a small swimming pool, and we made sure he wore a life jacket at the lake.

My children's protection was my highest priority. However, I could not protect Austin from a bullet. When that came my way, I did not know what to do. When I first saw his injury, I knew there was no way could "fix it" and help him. The injury was final.

However, I still prayed over him many times after I saw him. I guess tried to bring him back to me; I needed him.

At the hospital, when we saw him for the first time after the ambulance took him, we could not believe our wonderful boy was gone. We dropped to our knees at his bedside and wept; our hearts were broken, but we praised God for the wonderful, faithful little boy he became.

Austin was faithful to God. He taught us so many things about life —especially how important God was to him.

Trusting in the Lord gave me the strength to conquer another fear. Since getting married and having children, my fear of dying and leaving my family was my greatest fear. Since I lost my dad at a young age, I feared leaving my wife and children behind. I did not want to leave them alone.

Austin was the type of boy any dad would have been proud to carry on the family name. He was *my* boy—Austin Gabriel Haley. His mom gave him his first name, and I gave him his middle name. From the time he started showing little-boy tendencies, I could see myself in him.

When he would talk, run, or play, he looked and acted so much like me when I was a child.

He made me want to take an active role in being a dad. I will always make sure all my children realize they are loved by their dad, by telling them so. I will always miss my son, and I will never forget his example to me—how he lived and loved—and how much he told me so. It is a sign of strength, not weakness, for a man to express his love for his wife and children.

"This is my son, Austin, in whom I am well pleased." This is what I announced to his grandpa the day he was born. I handed Austin to him as I said those words to Renee's dad, Jack, knowing there would be a special relationship between Austin and him. I did not get to say those words to my own dad, but it was an honor to hand my son to his one living grandpa.

I would do anything for that boy. I gave him most things he asked for within reason because he showed us how much he loved us. The little things were what meant the most to Austin, so he didn't make many requests. He wanted to spend time with family.

On weekends, I would take my boys to the Saturday swap meet in Oklahoma City, and we had the greatest time. They would find the best toys. Austin was picky; he wanted the biggest bang for the buck. He knew what he wanted when he saw it, though.

He would pick up a toy, study it, and ask me what I thought. I'd tell him, "Whatever you want, Son; it's your choice." Sometimes we came out of there with a dozen toys and other times one. And that one toy would mean so much to him.

There were things I treasured about Austin. For example, he could run. He could run like no other child I had seen. I used to jog on the rack at the high school where we live, and his mama would walk him around with Dalton. Austin took off running behind me. At three years old, he ran a full lap around the track without stopping. It pleased me so much to see that in him. Oh, how I lived through my boy!

I was a track runner in school from junior high through high school. From time to time I have tried to get back into shape. Therefore, it pleased me to see my son running like the wind. If he saw me peeking out at him, he slowed as if I wasn't supposed to see how fast he was. He was humble.

He was not humble with girls, however. He loved girls, and they loved him. He had "girlfriends" like crazy—at school, at daycare, everywhere he went, even at the mall. If a girl, his age, spotted him and he spotted her, he wanted to know her name.

It's hard now to fathom that all I have are memories of him. Sure, I have some of his toys, some school papers showing his writing, pictures, and videos of him, but I know things will never be the same again. There will always be an empty place at the dinner table, an empty seat for the trip to the swap meet, and an empty space where Austin should be in his room playing with his little brother and other siblings.

I counted on Austin, and I know his mom and Dalton did, too. As we watched Austin grow, he was teaching, guiding, and protecting his little brother along the way. Dalton misses his big brother.

My dreams gave me special comfort. I often dwell on them because they have helped me along this journey. One dream, in particular, was a definite blessing. I saw a horse and a rider from a great distance. The rider was coming toward me, and I was in a large, open, fielded area like an enormous valley because we were surrounded by what seemed to be small hills.

As the rider came closer, I began to see it was Austin. He was still a little five-year-old boy, but he had a serious look on his face.

He was in full control of the horse, and I was amazed. The horse was reddish-brown, large, and powerful. When Austin turned the horse sideways, he made the horse rise on his hind legs. Austin revealed a large sword.

He wielded this sword as if he knew what he was doing. He returned the horse to all fours and rode away. It was an amazing, glorious, and powerful dream. I know the dream caused me to feel reassured of Austin's place in Heaven. He is now in the Lord's Army.

I haven't had a single nightmare, replaying the events of his death, and I thank God.

My hopes and prayers are that no one will ever have to experience what my wife and I have gone through with the loss of a family member. After facing the unexpected death of a child or someone close, a person is scarred for life. No one knows the pain except those who are in the small family of the unfortunate who has gone through the same loss.

I long to see in Heaven someday, all those who have gone on before me. I can imagine what it will be like on that reunion day. My family and I know that when the day comes, we will get to see our Savior, the one who holds our child in his protective arms and leads us out of the darkened days.

It is through Jesus alone that we can live today and have hope to overcome what tomorrow has in store.

Grandparents' Memories

NANNY'S THOUGHTS

Written by paternal grandmother, Bettie Haley:

I'll never forget the day Austin was born—Jack's first son. I held him in my arms, and as I looked at him, he looked at me. His eyes met mine as if he saw me. I knew there was something special about him.

As Austin grew, we all could see he had a special gift. By the time he was three years old, he showed concern and compassion for people. If he knew someone was sad, he was sorry. If they were sick, he would lay his tiny hands on them and ask Jesus to heal them, and he had perfect faith that they would be healed.

I loved going out to eat with Jack, Renee, and Austin because

Austin would sing. He had the sweetest voice, and he put feelings into a song as if he knew the meaning of the words. It was a joy to hear him.

It's hard for me to talk about Austin. I cherish all my grandchildren, but Austin was my soulmate, my kindred spirit. He was such a happy little boy.

One day they came to visit, and I heard him say, "Oh boy, we're at Nanny's, and we can do anything we want!" That thrilled my soul because I wanted him to enjoy coming to Nanny's house.

I am blessed that all the children still come to play, but it isn't the same. They miss him. He was a gentle leader, and they were drawn to him. They felt his love, his kindness. He was young, but he cared about them and prayed for them with a faith far beyond his years. I am so glad I am getting older. I won't have to wait so long to see him. I feel his love. It gets me through the long and lonesome days.

One of my most cherished memories was when I was sitting on a bench in my garden. I felt his little hand slip into mine. He sat beside me for a minute, and we listened to the wind chimes. He said in that sweet, clear voice, "I love you, Nanny. I love you, and I love your flowers." We hugged each other, and he ran off to play. I felt as if I was touched by an angel.

I could write a thousand thoughts and a thousand memories. But it hurts too much. When he passed away, it didn't only break my heart. It broke my soul. I am waiting for when God calls me. I know Austin will say, "Welcome home, Nanny. I love you." That will be Heaven for me.

GRANDMA'S THOUGHTS

Written by maternal grandmother, Cheryl Tracy:

Little Austin, oh, how I miss you; I remember the very moment you were born into this world on October 24, 2001. The first time I held you in my arms brought Grandma so much joy. You were such a beautiful little miracle of God with dark hair, dark eyes, and so perfect. There were so many family members there at the hospital we could not get into the room, but we all gathered around as your mama and daddy held you with such pride and joy as we sang the song, "Jesus Loves Me".

We always have lived next door to you, so we had the opportunity to watch you grow during the five years you were with us. My heart melted when I heard you say for the first time, "I love you, Grandma," and I would repeat the words back, "I love *you*, Austin."

I remember when you got to visit the church with us in Norman, Oklahoma. I can still hear your sweet little voice (at the age of three with a large vocabulary) when you sat beside me in the fellowship hall as we were eating a church dinner. I will never forget the treasured moment when you looked up and saw the hanging on the wall. "Grandma, there's a cross."

"Yes, baby, it is a cross."

You looked at me with your big, brown eyes. "Grandma, put your hand on your heart like this," as you placed your little hand on your own little heart. So, Grandma did as you suggested, and I placed my hand upon my heart. To my amazement, with a little louder voice, you began to preach like a little preacher: "Jesus lives right there in your

heart, and Jesus died for our sins; He shed his blood for us, and He died
so we can be saved."

Silence began to fill the room, as people were trying to hear this
little three-year-old boy tell me about Jesus. I treasure that moment
very much. Also, Grandma was so proud of you when we could visit
your church and how you would say your memory verse without ever
missing a word. You were a special little boy.

I remember all the many good times when Grandma had the oppor
tunity to go shopping with you at the mall. Sometimes, I would buy you
a little toy, give you a quarter to ride a few of the little rides or give you
a quarter to let you get gum out of the machine. It didn't matter how big
or small it was, your little eyes would light up with happiness. "Thank
you, Grandma," and you would give me a big hug. Everywhere we
went, you always wanted to have a Bible in your hand, even while you
were at the mall. You were always letting your little light shine for the
Lord.

I remember those times you were with us at Golden Corral restau
rant in Norman, Oklahoma when many of our family members would
meet there for a Sunday dinner after church. While we were all sitting
around the table, you would tell us the stories you learned while in your
Sunday-school class, taught by wonderful teachers, Don and Sandra
Colwell. We remember you telling us about a Bible story of Balaam and
the donkey. It was as though you were doing your best to tell the story
as your teacher told it, which made us all laugh when you began telling
us with expressive words and actions how God caused the donkey to
talk to Balaam.

I remember how I would run and play with you as we would play a
little game you made up. You would hold a little wand in your hand

and chase Grandma. When you got close to Grandma, you would point the wand toward me, and I would freeze and stand still. I would take the wand in my hand, and we would play the same game in reverse order. For some reason, I couldn't keep up with you, as you always would outrun Grandma.

I remember so many family gatherings when I would hear your laughter while playing with your little cousins. I also recall the five birthday parties when you blew out your candles as your little face lit up with such joy. I remind myself of the times I watched you anxiously open your Christmas gifts from under the Christmas tree.

Little Austin, my precious grandson, oh, how I miss you. I thank God for the treasured memories, which are such a comfort to Grandma. Almost every day I pick up your picture from my dresser, give you a kiss on the cheek, tell you how much I miss you and assure you Grandma will see you again, which somehow at that moment brings me closer to you.

I look forward to the day when we will all be reunited in Heaven. I long to see your little face, to hold you in my arms, and I hear your little voice say, "I love you, Grandma" and I say the words to you, "I love you, Austin."

Note from the Author:

I found this reflection of Austin saved on my dad's computer a few weeks after my dad passed away. God always seems to bring good things when times are so difficult.

GRANDPA'S THOUGHTS

Written by maternal grandfather, Jack Tracy I:

FIVE YEARS WITH AN ANGEL

From the time Austin was born, he was special. He was my first grandson, and I thought he was so handsome. But he had an inner beauty that was more important as he developed and grew older. He was a remarkable young man.

Austin was my little grandson. How I love him! He was the apple of my eye. He lived next door. When he came to see Cheryl and me, my storm door would bang as he hit it at full speed. He ran in as fast his legs would carry him and grabbed me around the leg, saying, ``I love you, Grandpa." He was so special to me.

He was not my first grandchild, but he was my first grandson. When he was born, he looked like his dad. He had a full head of dark brown hair and dark brown eyes. I thought he was handsome.

When Austin was born, we stood in the delivery suite and gathered round to welcome Austin into the family. Jack, Renee's husband, placed little Austin in my arms. There he lay in my arms—as perfect as can be.

Jack and Renee prayed for Austin before he was born and asked

God to keep him and protect him. In her heart and Jack's heart, they gave Austin to the Lord before and after he was born.

As he grew older, it was clear Austin was a gifted child. He could memorize Bible passages at a young age. Renee is a Nationally Certified English Teacher, and she spent a lot of time teaching him to read. They sat and read book after book, but his favorite book was the Bible. He worked hard to learn his memory verses.

Almost every Sunday we would meet Renee and their family at Golden Corral. Austin loved to tell us the Bible teachings he learned in Sunday school.

I remember him telling me about Balaam in his own words. "God told Balaam not to go. Balaam went anyway. The angel was going to kill Balaam," he explained, as he motioned with his hands. "The donkey mashed Balaam's foot and laid on the ground. Balaam hit him like this," he continued showing me the motions. "Grandpa, the donkey turned around, and looked right at Balaam and asked, 'Why did you hit me?'" Austin was a little evangelist. He always prayed, all his life. His desire was for others to come to know Jesus. It seemed as though he was always thinking of others.

I will always remember how he ran at full blast everywhere he went. He was so full of energy. He loved his little brother and nurtured and hovered over him. He loved his mom and dad, grandparents, and friends.

One of the greatest legacies is his love of God. He expressed his love of God almost every day. He prayed for his family, including me.

He was destined to be a preacher, teacher, prophet, or evangelist. He was my little man.

I loved him with all my heart. One of his last prayers was for my healing, and God answered his prayer!

Austin did everything with Dalton. He was the best big brother, and they played together all the time. Austin liked to be the one to get Dalton up in the morning. Dalton would wake to Austin caressing and loving on him. When Dalton got up, Austin would snuggle up on the couch, take his favorite blanket, and cover both of them with it. They turned on movies and watched television together.

When Dalton went to bed at night, Austin was there to help him say his prayers and tuck him in for the night. He loved Dalton and made every effort to keep Dalton happy.

I taught Austin and my other grandchildren a few good things. Early on, I showed my grandchildren a one-dollar bill and told them that was *my* picture on it. When I asked them whose picture was on the dollar, they would declare it was "Grandpa." I would give it to them.

They looked at the dollar bill in awe, and they believed every word of the story. This was great fun, too, as I gave them several dollar bills throughout the years. They knew Grandpa almost always had one for them.

I can't believe that when Austin started school, his school teachers tried to tell them George Washington's picture was on the bill. They should be re-educated, "What did that teacher know anyway," I would roar.

Of course, those were *one*-dollar bills.

One day, someone wanted to give one of my grandchildren a *five*-dollar bill. Austin handed it back as it didn't have "Grandpa's picture." He didn't want a five-dollar bill. He wanted a genuine "grandpa-dollar bill".

A few days before Austin passed away, Renee heard him praying "I love you, God. I love you, Jesus. I love you, Holy Spirit." He asked "Mama, when am I going to be filled with the Holy Spirit?" He was a true God chaser, and he often expressed his love for God.

He carried his Bible or Bibles with him about everywhere he went He preached to his friends. In fact, Austin wanted to take several Bibles to the mall or other shopping places, and Renee had to tell him to take *one* Bible when they went inside the stores, so he would carefully select the one he wanted. At times, she would let him bring all five in the store because he wanted to so badly. He would clutch the Bibles and say, "Now, I'm in the Lord's army." As a boy, he would want footballs and toys, and he loved puzzles, but he was unusual because he loved Bibles the most.

I remember when months before the tragedy he was visiting the church my wife and I attend. He saw a cross on the wall that was there to decorate our back room. He told Cheryl, "Grandma, Jesus died on a cross."

Grandma said kindly, "Yes, he did."

"Grandma," he urged her, "put your hand right here," he motioned by putting his hand over his heart. "Jesus lives in here."

He took Grandma's hand and placed it over her heart and said "Right here, Grandma." "Yes, he does live there."

Austin and I loved to go to my pond—our pond. It was our refuge It is secluded by some trees, but not too many. It is stocked with catfish and we loved to go there to feed them. This was one of our lovely times together.

Even before Austin was old enough to walk, we took him to a fishing dock we built on the water. He would run around on the lock, and I was worried about him falling in the water as he would run fast toward the edge of the dock and throw out fish food as far as he could. I held his hand to keep him from getting too close to the side.

As he grew older, I went to his house about two hundred yards away on a golf cart. I called it a "goof" cart. Later, I bought an ATV and continued to pick up Austin and his brother, Dalton. I let him stand and guide the "goof" cart as we wandered toward the pond about another two hundred feet away.

It was a great time. All of us enjoyed the outing. We would throw out fish food and maybe catch a fish. It was such a peaceful place at the pond. When he threw out the food, the water would swirl with dozens of catfish as they hustled for the food.

At times, I helped him catch a fish or two. I loved to watch the fish run with Austin struggling to hold the pole. It was our time together. We spent good times there, several times a week. Little did we know, Austin's time was short, and our days together were numbered.

I think of our last few minutes together. He wanted to go fishing at our pond. It was one of the joys of life we liked to share. We went to the pond to feed the fish and catch one. Little did we know he had minutes to live. As tragic as his death was, I am glad I was with him to the end and held him in his death as I clutched him and struggled to carry him up the hill to the four-wheeler. I prayed there could be some miracle to save his life, but it was not so. I wanted to die. I felt like I was responsible for the death of my little grandson.

I felt as if a huge cross was laid on my back, and I could hardly carry it. I was overwhelmed! I struggled to make it a minute at a time. I wanted to die, too! Why not me, I reasoned? I had Hepatitis C, and my liver was almost gone. I had a stroke and was almost dead anyway. Why didn't the bullet hit me?

But it was not so. My precious grandson . . . I will cherish the memories of the fish we caught, our memories together, and the love we shared for life.

I have not slept well since Austin's death. I sleep many nights on the couch. It seems I relive the whole incident and dream about hearing the shot that killed him. I see him lying on the dock and his eyes looking at me asking me to help him. I want to help him, but there is nothing can do. I reach for him, but I can't help him. I carry him in my dreams but I can't help him no matter how much I try. I wake up in a cold sweat missing him so much.

I often read this verse found in Philippians 4:8: "Finally, brethren, whatsoever things are true, whatsoever things are honest, whatsoever things are just, whatsoever things are pure, whatsoever things are lovely, whatsoever things are of good report; if there be any virtue, and if there be any praise, think on these things."

We must find time to focus on the good things of life as much as possible when we are overwhelmed with grief. Think and focus on the good things you shared together. Try hard. I was recently thinking about the life Austin lived, and I have also had dreams at times that was entering the gates of Heaven.

There I saw Austin running to meet me as he did in my living room. He was throwing his little arms around my leg again, and we shared our love together again. You see, this is not always going to be a dream.

It may seem like it is a long way off, but it isn't. In the limitless time of eternity, it is around the corner. I have one more person to go to Heaven for.

As for now on Earth, I have several other grandchildren. I want to enjoy them and love them. They need me, and they need comfort, too. In these times of grief, families must band together, love one another, and support one another—right down to the youngest in our family. Don't forget the little ones. They need your love and kindness. They grieve, too.

I want to tell you something about love. You must give it away. The more love you give away, the more love comes back to you. It isn't lost by giving it away, it is multiplied. The word "love" appears 310 times in the King James Version of the Bible. We are instructed to love God, and he tells us how much he loves us over and over. How much we should follow his example and tell our family and friends how much we love them.

As a Sunday school teacher, I knew Christians who shared with me that they were not able to tell their children they love them. What a loss! I hope you will tell your children every day you love them. Tell your companion you love him or her, then go on and show them you do. Do something kind or thoughtful for them.

Thankfully, death is not the end for the Christian. It is merely a passing to a new place to live, a much better place. I remembered the words of my dad as he came nearer to the end of his days. We were sitting in his pickup watching cars drive the highway. "Son, do you see that car going over the hill?"

"Yes," I replied.

"Now the car has disappeared over the hill, and you can't see it anymore, right?"

"Yeah," I agreed.

We approached the top of the hill. "Now, you can see the car again, can't you?" He said, "That's the way death is. Before long, I will go over the hill and you won't see me again until you go over the hill." Our hope and promise are that we will all be reunited again! It wasn't too many years before Dad made the trip over the hill. Now, Austin has too, but I purpose in my heart to meet him again. What a reunion it will be!

I can imagine the happy reunion in Heaven along with my other family and friends. After all, there will be a Tree of Life in Heaven, and the Bible speaks of it in the book of Revelation. That tree of life has healing in its leaves. Once I make it to Heaven, I will be restored. My body will no longer be broken. Oh, how I look forward to that day. What a day that will be!

I know Austin is waiting for me at Heaven's gates. I long to see him, to hold him, and to be able to express my love to him again. I want to kiss him again and enjoy spending time with him in a whole, healed body. I'll be able to run fast and keep up with him. Yes, Heaven will be wonderful. I expect the River of Life will have fish for us to catch. I will see him again. Heaven is our blessed hope!

Note from the Author:

Unfortunately, we had to say goodbye to my grandma nine months after my dad passed away; she passed from this life on Earth on March 20, 2022. I'm thankful we will see her in Heaven someday. What a reunion it will be.

MAMAW'S THOUGHTS

Written by maternal great-grandmother, Dixie Gillum:

REMEMBERING MY PRECIOUS LITTLE GREAT-GRANDSON, AUSTIN HALEY

It brought us such joy when we received the call on October 24, 2001, from Jack, Austin's daddy. He was taking Renee to the hospital because it was time for Austin to be born. The excitement was in the air as both sides of the family stood in the hallway, waiting to hear that first little cry from Jack and Renee's firstborn son. How happy we all were; we stood around the bed when the nurse let us in and sang, "Jesus Loves Me," as we do with all the babies born in our family. It was a precious and sacred moment as Jack Haley handed Jack Tracy little Austin and said, "This is my son in whom I am well pleased." It brought tears to everyone there. As I held Austin, I felt such warmth come over me; I knew he was special, and God had His hand upon him.

What a special little boy he became as he got older—the joy he brought to all our family. Austin loved to fish with his grandpa, Jack, and great-grandpa, Jim. His great-grandpa would bait his hook and play with him often. Austin would get excited when he caught a fish. When we had our family dinners, he loved playing with his cousins so much. enjoyed sitting and listening to them all laugh and play games.

All the children were close to one another. Words cannot express how blessed we all were because of Austin. It was plain to see how God had his hand upon him. No matter where we went, he always talked about Jesus. At two and three years of age, he wanted to carry his Bible at times one in each hand. Austin saw a one-way sign on the side of the road while on the way to the mall. He said, "Mama, that sign reminds me of the song, 'One Way, Jesus!'" He had the sweetest little voice ye spoke with such depth and wisdom.

Austin's little brother, Dalton, who was two at the time, would ge Austin's attention sometimes by lovingly hitting Austin so he would play with him. One time, Dalton hit a little too hard, not realizing how hard he was hitting since he was so young. Austin was always so kind to his little brother, and this time he said, "Little brother, don't hit too hard. Bubba loves you." Austin always loved and helped his little brother. He even helped potty train Dalton by playing with him and bragging about him every day.

The short five years we were blessed to have him on this Earth wil never be forgotten. We will see our little boy with the sweet little voice again. I can almost hear him say, "I love you, MaMaw. I would reply, ' love you, Austin.'"

The loss of a child is noted to be the worst pain anyone can experi ence. I could relate to Jack and Renee and their pain of losing their first born son, Austin. I lost my son, Michael W. Lee, my firstborn son (Renee Haley's uncle) because of a fatal car wreck when he was only twenty-one years old.

Tragedy

God is the answer to any trial we face. "The Lord is close to the brokenhearted and saves those who are crushed in spirit; a righteous man may have many troubles, but the Lord delivers him out of them all" (Psalms 34:18-19). We miss our precious little boy. Heaven is sweeter now.

Appendix

Comforting Bible Verses during Grief and Sadness

The Lord also will be a refuge for the oppressed, a refuge in times o
trouble.

Psalm: 9:9

The Lord is my rock and my fortress and my deliverer; my God, my
strength, in whom I will trust; my shield and the horn of my salvation
my stronghold.

Psalm 18:2

For he has not despised nor abhorred the affliction of the afflicted; no
has He hidden his face from Him; But when He cried to Him, He
heard.

Psalm 22:24

The Lord is my shepherd; I shall not want. He makes me to lie down in
green pastures; he leads me beside the still waters. He restores my soul

He leads me in the paths of righteousness for his name's sake. Yea, though I walk through the valley of the shadow of death, I will fear no evil; for you are with me; Your rod and Your staff, they comfort me. You prepare a table before me in the presence of my enemies; You anoint my head with oil; my cup runs over. Surely goodness and mercy shall follow me all the days of my life; and I will dwell in the house of the Lord forever.

Psalm 23

One thing I have desired of the Lord, that will I seek: that I may dwell in the house of the Lord all the days of my life, to behold the beauty of the Lord and to inquire in his temple. For in the day of trouble He shall hide me in His pavilion; in the secret place of His tabernacle he shall hide me; He shall set me upon a high rock.

Psalm 27:4-5

Weeping may endure for a night, but joy comes in the morning.

Psalm 30:5

The Lord is near to those who have a broken heart, and saves such as have a contrite spirit.

Psalm 34:18

The salvation of the righteous is from the Lord; He is their strength in the time of trouble.

Psalm 37:39

God is our refuge and strength, a very present help in trouble. Therefore, we will not fear, even though the earth be removed, and though the mountains be carried into the midst of the sea.

Psalm 46:1-2

For this is God, our God for ever and ever; He will be our guide even to death.

Psalm 48:14

Tragedy

Cast your burden on the Lord and He shall sustain you; He shall never permit the righteous to be moved.

Psalm 55:22

You who have shown me severe and great troubles, shall revive me again, and bring me up again from the depths of the earth. You shall increase my greatness, and comfort me on every side.

Psalm 71: 20-21

My flesh and my heart may fail, but God is the strength of my heart and my portion forever.

Psalm 73:26

Though I walk in the midst of trouble, you will revive me; you will stretch out your hand against the wrath of my enemies, and your right hand will save me.

Psalm 138:7

He will swallow up death forever, and the Lord God will wipe away tears from all faces; the rebuke of His people He will take away from all the earth; for the Lord has spoken.

Isaiah 25:8

Have you not known? Have you not heard? The everlasting God, the Lord, the creator of the ends of the earth, neither faints nor is weary. His understanding is unsearchable. He gives power to the weak, and to those who have no might He increases strength. Even the youths shall faint and be weary, and the young men shall utterly fall, but those who wait on the Lord shall renew their strength; they shall mount up with wings like eagles, they shall run and not be weary, they shall walk and not faint.

Isaiah 40:28-31

But Zion said, "The Lord has forsaken me, and my Lord has forgotten me." Can a woman forget her nursing child, and not have compassion on the son of her womb? Surely they may forget, yet I will not forget you. See, I have inscribed you on the palms of My hands; your walls are continually before Me.

Isaiah 49:14-16

For the Lord will comfort Zion, He will comfort all her waste places; he will make her wilderness like Eden, and her desert like the garden of he Lord; joy and gladness will be found in it, thanksgiving and the voice of melody.

Isaiah 51:3

For the mountains shall depart and the hills be removed, but my kindness shall not depart from you, nor shall my covenant of peace be emoved, says the Lord, who has mercy on you.

Isaiah 54:10

For thus says the Lord: Behold, I will extend peace to her like a river, and the glory of the Gentiles like a flowing stream. Then you shall feed; on her sides shall you be carried, and be dandled on her knees. As one whom his mother comforts, so I will comfort you; and you shall be comforted in Jerusalem.

Isaiah 66:12-14

For the Lord will not cast off forever. Though He causes grief, yet He will show compassion according to the multitude of His mercies. For He does not afflict willingly, nor grieve the children of men.

Lamentations 3:31-33

I will ransom them from the power of the grave; I will redeem them from death. O Death, I will be your plagues! O Grave, I will be your destruction! Pity is hidden from My eyes.

Hosea 13:14

The Lord is good, a stronghold in the day of trouble; and He knows those who trust in Him.

Nahum 1:7

Blessed are those who mourn, for they shall be comforted.

Matthew 5:4

Do not lay up for yourselves treasures on earth, where moth and rust destroy and where thieves break in and steal; but lay up for yourselves treasures in heaven, where neither moth nor rust destroys and where thieves do not break in and steal. For where your treasure is, there your heart will be also.

Matthew 6:19-21

Come to Me, all you who labor and are heavy laden, and I will give you rest. Take My yoke upon you and learn from Me, for I am gentle and lowly in heart, and you will find rest for your souls. For My yoke is easy and My burden is light.
Matthew 11:28-30

This is the will of the Father who sent Me, that of all He has given Me I should lose nothing, but should raise it up at the last day. And this is the

will of Him who sent Me, that everyone who sees the Son and believes
in Him may have everlasting life; and I will raise him up at the last day.

John 6:39-40

Let not your heart be troubled; you believe in God, believe also in Me.
In my Father's house are many mansions; if it were not so, I would have
told you. I go to prepare a place for you, and if I go and prepare a place
for you, I will come again and receive you to Myself; that where I am,
there you may be also. And where I go you know, and the way you
know.

John 14:1-4

Peace I leave with you; my peace I give to you; not as the world gives do
I give to you. Let not your heart be troubled, neither let it be afraid.

John 14:27

For as many as are led by the Spirit of God, these are sons of God. For
you did not receive the spirit of bondage again to fear, but you received
the Spirit of adoption by whom we cry out, "Abba, Father."

Tragedy

What then shall we say to these things? If God is for us, who can be against us? He who did not spare His own Son, but delivered Him up for us all, how shall He not with Him also freely give us all things? Who shall bring a charge against God's elect? It is God who justifies. Who is he who condemns? It is Christ who died, and furthermore is also risen, who is even at the right hand of God, who also makes intercession with us. Who shall separate us from the love of Christ? Shall tribulation, or distress, or persecution, or famine, or nakedness, or peril, or sword? As it is written: For Your sake we are killed all day long; we are accounted as sheep for the slaughter. Yet in all of those things we are more than conquerors through Him who loved us. For I am persuaded that neither death nor life, nor angels nor principalities nor powers, nor things present nor things to come, nor height nor depth, nor any other created thing, shall be able to separate us from the love of God which is in Christ Jesus our Lord.

Romans 8:31-39

In a moment, in the twinkling of an eye, at the last trumpet. For the trumpet will sound, and the dead will be raised incorruptible, and we shall be changed. For this corruption must put on incorruption, and this mortal must put on immortality. So when this corruptible has put on incorruption, and this mortal has put on immortality, then shall be brought to pass the saying that is written: "Death is swallowed up in victory." O Death, where is your sting? O Hades, where is your victory? The sting of death is sin, and the strength of sin is the law. But thanks be to God, who gives us the victory through our Lord Jesus Christ.

I Corinthians 15:52-57

Blessed be the God and Father of our Lord Jesus Christ, the Father of mercies and God of all comfort, who comforts us in all our tribulation, that we may be able to comfort those who are in , with the comfort with which we ourselves are comforted by God. For as the sufferings of Christ abound in us, so our consolation also abounds through Christ.

II Corinthians 1:3-5

According to what is written, "I believed and therefore I spoke," we also believe and therefore speak, knowing that He who raised up the Lord Jesus will also raise us up with Jesus, and will present us with you. For all things are for your sakes, that grace, having spread through the many, may cause thanksgiving to abound to the glory of God. Therefore, we do not lose heart. Even though our outward man is perishing, yet the inward man is being renewed day by day.

Tragedy

II Corinthians 4:13-16

And he said to me, "My grace is sufficient for you, for my strength is made perfect in weakness." Therefore, most gladly I will rather boast in my infirmities, that the power of Christ may rest upon me. Therefore, I take pleasure in infirmities, in reproaches, in needs, in persecutions, in distresses, for Christ's sake. For when I am weak, then I am strong.

II Corinthians 12:9-10

Be anxious for nothing, but in everything by prayer and supplication, with thanksgiving, let your requests be made known to God.

Philippians 4:6

But I do not want you to be ignorant, brethren, concerning those who have fallen asleep, lest you sorrow as others who have no hope.

I Thessalonians 4:13

Since the children have flesh and blood, he too shared in their humanity so that by his death he might destroy him who holds the power of death—that is, the devil—and free those who all their lives were held in slavery by their fear of death.

Hebrews 2:14-15

Inasmuch then as the children have partaken of flesh and blood, He Himself likewise shared in the same, that through death He might destroy him who had the power of death, that is, the devil, and release those who through fear of death were all their lifetime subject to bondage. For indeed He does not give aid to angels, but He does give aid to the seed of Abraham.

Hebrews 4:14-16

Blessed be the God and Father of our Lord Jesus Christ, who according to His abundant mercy has begotten us again to a living hope through the resurrection of Jesus Christ from the dead, to an inheritance incorruptible and undefiled and that does not fade away, reserved in heaven for you, who are kept by the power of God through faith for salvation ready to be revealed in the last time. In this you greatly rejoice, though now for a little while, if need be, you have been grieved by various trials, that the genuineness of your faith, being much more precious han gold that perishes, though it is tested by fire, may be found to praise, honor, and glory at the revelation of Jesus Christ, whom having not seen you love. Though now you do not see Him, yet believing, you rejoice with joy inexpressible and full of glory, receiving the end of your faith the salvation of your souls.

I Peter 1:3-9

Therefore, humble yourselves under the mighty hand of God, that he may exalt you in due time, casting all your care upon Him, for He cares for you.

I Peter 5:6-7

And God will wipe away every tear from their eyes; there shall be no more death, nor sorrow, nor crying. There shall be no more pain, for the former things have passed away.

Revelation 21:4

Unforgettable Quotes from Family and Friends

Dalton (brother) when waking up on Austin's birthday: "Mama, today is Austin's birthday, and they are having a big party for him in Heaven. I want to go—I promise I will come back" (age three).

Gabriel (brother): I was only born nine months after you passed away. I wish I could have known you. I'll see you in Heaven (age thirteen).

Mikayla (sister): Hello, I'm Austin's sister. I never saw Austin, but I feel like I know a lot about him. He tells God to make sure my family's safe. I know I'll see him someday, but I still cry a lot because I don't get to see him. I know Austin would want me to be happy, so I will. (age 10)

Mikayla (sister): I wish I knew Austin, and I hope I dream about him someday (age ten).

Dalton to Grandma Cheryl: "Grandma, I have a puzzle of all the states that I put together. Would you show me where Heaven is on my puzzle?" (age three)

Cheryl (grandma): "Austin went from the joy of fishing with his grandpa into the arms of Jesus."

. . .

Cheryl: "I can't put my finger on it, but this child is very, very special because of all the things Austin has said regarding his deep love for God at such a young age."

Cheryl: "Our grandbaby. Why? Why? Why?" (falling to her knees)

Bettie (grandma): "It's murder in my opinion."

Bettie: "I miss the hugs and kisses I would get from Austin. He was such a special little boy."

Dixie (great-grandma): "Austin, baby, you never cease to amaze me—the beautiful things you say about Jesus."

Dixie: "Austin, God's got His hand on you, sweetheart. God is going to use you one day."

Michelle's (aunt) Intercessory Prayer: "God, place the burden on me that my sister is carrying so she can make it through this difficult time of losing her son. Allow me to help carry the load." (Michelle was heavily burdened for a long time).

. . .

Sandy (aunt): "I had the opportunity to babysit Austin for a couple of years. We would often sing the song from Petra called "We Need Jesus" together in the car. I still remember his little voice singing along, "And we shall live forever . . . when we share the love of Jesus." We spent many times watching his favorite television shows: *Sesame Street*, *Dora the Explorer*, and *Bob the Builder*. I'm better for having known him—we all are.""

Barbara (aunt): "He would always run through the door and give me a smile of recognition when he was coming to my shop to get his hair trimmed.""

Travis (uncle): "God, I know You are dealing with me about some things and You were trying to get my attention, but, God, not this!""

Justin (cousin): "God is going to use Austin's situation to touch people's lives all over the world.""

Baylie (cousin): "Austin is in Heaven, and he is so happy" (three years old).

Carson Howlett (friend): "Austin was my very, very best friend. I love him so much. He is in Heaven, and I miss him" (age seven).

. . .

Colin Deaton (friend): "Austin was nice, and I remember playing T-ball with him" (age seven).

Jackson Pensoneau (friend): "Austin was my very best friend. We liked to play with each other. We had a good time together. Austin got shot, and he died. I feel really, really sad about it. Austin is happy in Heaven. He's eating a big ice cream sundae" (age seven).

Seth Tennison (friend): "Austin was my best friend. I miss him very much" (age seven).

Noah Standridge (friend): "Austin was a really good friend. I liked to play blocks with him. Austin was kind and honest" (age seven).

About the Author

f you found encouragement from this book, please pass it on or
ourchase a copy for someone else in need of hope. Also, Renee Haley
would be grateful if you write a review on Amazon and/or social media.

Renee Haley and her husband, Jack, reside in Noble, Oklahoma, with their three children. After the loss of their son was broadcasted throughout the United States and around the world, Renee has developed a passion for uplifting and encouraging others who have also experienced the heartache of losing a child or faced an unimaginable situation.

Renee and her husband have been married for twenty-three years and are the parents of Austin (forever 5), Dalton (age 18), Gabriel (age 14), and Mikayla (age 11).

Renee graduated from the University of Science and Arts of Oklahoma and received a Bachelor's Degree in Elementary Education. She also obtained her Master's Degree in Public School Administration from East Central University. Renee has taught middle school English Language Arts for twenty-four years and has received her National Board Certification.

Renee Haley's story has been published in newspapers and aired on news stations locally, nationally, and internationally with ABC, CBS, NBC, FOX, and PBS. Their family's story has also been addressed on the front page of *The Norman Transcript*, *The Oklahoman*, *Tulsa World*, and *USA Today*.

Renee and her husband were interviewed on several of the news programs as well as TBN, the *Trinity Broadcasting Network*. It has also been written for such publications as *Today's Pentecostal Evangel*, *ATA World Magazine*, and other leading periodicals. A music composer, Chris Rogerson, wrote an award-winning orchestral piece entitled Noble Pond, about Austin's loss: www.chrisrogerson.com/works/noble pond.

Over the past few years, Renee has shared Austin's story in various churches, and many police stations across the United States use their story in the training of new officers.

More information at:
https://reneehaley.com

Facebook Group: Christian Prayer, Praise, and Restore

Endnotes

Emerson, L. O. *Jesus Loves Me.* Ditson & Co., Oliver, Boston, monographic, 1873. Notated Music. https://www.loc.gov/item/sm1873.11629/.

Made in United States
Orlando, FL
11 September 2024